BUSINESS PLANS
THAT GET
INVESTMENT

A REAL-WORLD GUIDE ON HOW TO
WRITE A BUSINESS PLAN

DAVID BATEMAN

In collaboration with Oxford Investment Opportunity Network Ltd

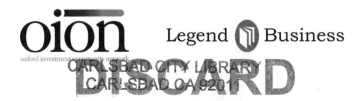

oion
oxford investment opportunity network

Legend Business

Legend Business, 175-185 Gray's Inn Road, London, WC1X 8UE
info@legend-paperbooks.co.uk | www.legendpress.co.uk

British Library Cataloguing in Publication Data available.

Print ISBN 978-1-7850793-2-0
Ebook ISBN 978-1-7850793-3-7
Set in Times. Printed in the United Kingdom by Clays Ltd.
Cover design by Robert Harries

Legend Business

CONTENTS

SPONSOR INFORMATION

Business Plans That Get Investment is sponsored by The Oxford Investment Opportunity Network (OION, www.oion.co.uk).

The Oxford Investment Opportunity Network was established in 1994 as one of the UK's first business angel networks. OION has an interest in companies with a strong barrier to entry, often patented and a spin-out from research, but any company with a strong vision for growth will be considered to present to the Network. Today, OION is one of the UK's most successful technology focused business angel networks, linking investors to companies with high growth potential seeking investment from less than £200k to £1.5 million.

OION has also formed two other successful investment networks; The Thames Valley Investment Network (TVIN, www.tvin.co.uk) for companies with a focus on media, including FMCG, lifestyle and green-technology; and Oxford Early Investments (OEI, www.oxei.co.uk) for earlier stage investment opportunities, often where more than just investment is being sought. OEI is suitable for companies seeking from £75k up to £250k and often where the new government Seed Enterprise Investment Scheme (SEIS) scheme is relevant.

FOREWORD

Oxford Investment Opportunity Network (OION) is one of the UK's largest and most well-established angel networks. At OION we introduce entrepreneurs and business owners to a range of investors, with a view to investment.

As OION's Investment Network Manager I have received and reviewed thousands of business plans over the years. A constant hurdle that I face is that all too often a potentially sound, or even great, business idea is presented in a confused and lengthy state. With key points and investment criteria missing, such plans could potentially lose an otherwise great opportunity for investment backing. Consequently, we spend many hours prior to an investment meeting helping entrepreneurs to get their business plans into a clear and direct format, ready for presentation and pitch to our network member investors.

Business Plans that Get Investment addresses the key criteria that an investor needs to be able to make an assessment of a business plan and the corresponding investment proposal. It does this with a very straightforward, yet comprehensive, methodology and tackles the essential points that are required for investment.

Based on my experience with OION, I firmly believe that if you are an entrepreneur or businessperson who is seriously considering raising investment, you should read this book and take on board the structure and advice within; it will significantly improve your chances of attracting initial interest that could lead to investment success and enable you to take your business to the next stage of growth.

**—Eileen Modral, Investment Network Manager,
Oxford Investment Opportunity Network**

PART 1

LAYING THE FOUNDATIONS

CHAPTER 1. INTRODUCTION

Ask any entrepreneur why they need a business plan, and they will say: to attract new investment to my business, so that it can grow.

But business plans are often a cause of great stress and concern for those who write them. Justifiably so: get it right and you can secure your investment and grow your business; get it wrong and you may blow your chances of success.

So what is a business plan?

Your business plan is the medium that you use to communicate to potential investors what your business does and how they will be able to make money from it. You should think of it as an 'investment pitch'. It should give potential investors a clear understanding of how they can benefit from the future growth of your business. A business plan is all about putting yourself in an investor's shoes, and focussing on their agenda, rather than your own.

Investors' needs

What makes writing a business plan so difficult is that no standard formula exists, which leaves you second-guessing what a potential investor wants to see. This book shows you how to put a plan together that has precisely the information an investor needs. This will enable them to take that essential first step towards an informed investment decision.

Dragons' Den is a popular TV series in which aspiring entrepreneurs present their business ideas to a panel of successful, multi-millionaire investors. If the panellists like the idea, they invest in the business. Most of the people who present to the Dragons seem to fail. Even if they have a credible idea, it is often clear that the business itself has not been properly thought through. Those who do succeed are invariably well prepared, giving clear and concise answers to the probing questions of the Dragons. Crucially, their questions are often the same for each new presentation:

'What's your background?'
'How does this product work?'
'How much does it cost to produce?'
'How many have you sold?'
'How much money have you put into it?'
'Do you own the intellectual property?'
'How much investment do you need?'
'How will you spend my investment?'
... and so on.

Clearly, *Dragons' Den* is produced largely for entertainment purposes, but it is striking how relevant the business questions it throws up are to the business plan that you will need in order to successfully pitch for investment. If you want to know what an investor needs, and therefore what you must say in your own business plan, you could do worse than simply watching a few episodes. The questions that you hear on the show are likely to be the same as those that your business plan must address – and your aim must be to answer them before they are asked.

The fundamental point is this: if you don't know what you should be saying in the first place, or what investors want to hear, it's effectively impossible to get it down on paper. I learned this indispensable lesson the hard way. But it doesn't have to be that way for you.

Keep it simple

Contrary to popular opinion, a business plan should always be concise and simple. It does not require excessive detail or reams of numbers. Likewise, the process of creating a plan need not be difficult or complicated.

In this book I will show you how to write an effective, professional business plan of no more than fourteen pages, with as few as ten sentences per page! By working to the structure revealed in this book your plan will take no more than a few days to write, at the very most.

When writing business plans, many people feel compelled to overburden them with words and information, believing that will make them seem weightier and more impressive. This is absolutely the wrong approach. In fact, the opposite is true: the fewer words the better. This is an area in which less is definitely more. You need to think of writing your plan as something similar to writing a song: you don't have endless space to fill, because of the constraints on the length and structure of the song. You are forced to express yourself in a compressed space, often using very few words. An ideal business plan will follow the same principles, stating only what is absolutely necessary.

One size fits all

The business plan structure that is outlined in this book applies to almost any kind of business, irrespective of its size, what it does or how much money it makes. It is a universal, 'one-size-fits-all' methodology.

Your business might be anything from a raw, entrepreneurial start-up to a well-established, multi-million-pound firm that employs hundreds of people. In either case, the challenge is the same: you will need to raise investment money, typically with the aim of growing your business and taking it to the next level. The only real variation is in the size of the investment you need, and who you would approach for the money.

The same principles apply to a business plan whatever the type and size of the business it is for. Specific content and other details will of course vary from one type of business to another, but the fundamental structure and objectives will be remarkably consistent across all businesses.

I recently saw a business plan for a manufacturer of a hair-removal laser. The company was looking to raise a seven-figure investment. It struck me how similar the layout and key points of this plan were to one I had co-written many years earlier, for an asset-management business that was aiming to raise more than a billion dollars. You might think that such a business could hardly be more different from a laser hair-removal company, and that there is a big difference between a million pounds and a billion dollars. Yet the plans were uncannily similar, with the titles of each page and the overall structure being broadly consistent.

Based on experience

The approach in this book is borne out of many years' direct experience. I have actually written plans and secured investment on numerous occasions.

Moreover, I have seen it from both sides of the fence: I have been both entrepreneur and investor. The amounts involved ranged from just tens of thousands of pounds for my first business, through to hundreds of millions of dollars of investors' capital, later in my career. By this stage I had become an investor myself, and received hundreds of plans every year asking for financial backing. During that time I was able to observe at first-hand what worked and what didn't. Experience taught me what caught an investor's eye and what got sent to the bottom of the pile.

My first attempt at writing a business plan was, quite naturally, a disaster. The business I had started was a software company, and was being carried along by the frenzy of the dotcom boom of the late nineties. I knew what I wanted to do and where I wanted to take my business. 'So put it down in a business plan and go and raise some money' was my mentor's sound but succinct advice. Not as easy as it might sound. I agonised over the process of writing the business plan for many weeks. I read books and got 'expert' advice, but there was still no light at the end of the tunnel. It all just seemed so complicated.

This was a fairly brutal learning process for someone who fancied he could take this kind of task in his stride. After all, I had read languages at Cambridge, was comfortable when it came to putting pen to paper, and had later attended the Management Studies course at the University's business school. (Incidentally, the Management Studies syllabus at that time had nothing to say about writing business plans!)

In the end, I muddled through and managed to raise early-stage investment – no thanks to the shoddy and disjointed document that I referred to as my 'business plan'. My plan lacked structure, was far too verbose, failed to address the key points that an investor needs to understand, and was simply not clear about what I was trying to achieve. I cringe now when I realise how hard I made things for myself and how much easier and more efficient the whole process could have been had someone shown me the right approach.

Years later, I was working in the financial sector, starting out on London's City trading floors. After selling the software business I vowed that I would never again start a business without ready access to the elusive capital needed to create a successful venture. My logic was that if I wanted access to money, I would go and work with people who control the money – and that meant the world of finance.

Inevitably, as with so many careful life-plans, things went a little off-course and took longer than expected. At that time the financial sector was a great place not only for learning about business at the sharp end, but also for making good money. After several years in the manic environment of trading floors, I joined a team that was starting a hedge fund: a type of business that was then very much in vogue, in which spectacular fortunes were being made – and lost.

The business was launched with the backing of a large European investment bank. I was a partner in it and one of my responsibilities included putting together all of the marketing material that we would present to potential investors – and crucially this included the business plan (known in the industry, somewhat fancifully, as the 'marketing presentation').

Over several weeks the plan went through many stages until the finished version was ready. As a team, our experience in finance meant that we had seen enough plans by then to know what was likely to excite an investor's interest. The plan was clear and concise, and covered all the areas that an investor would need to understand about our business. We used this plan in the early days to present to investors and showcase our fund, with the aim that they would decide to invest money with us.

Over the course of the following four years we raised nearly four billion dollars of investment for the fund, taking us into the top ten European hedge funds at one point. Not a bad result! The business plan stood the test of time: although its details have changed here and there over the years, its fundamental structure and message remain intact from the original document that was drafted.

Just to be clear, I am not for a moment suggesting that securing such an enormous investment was solely the result of a well-constructed business plan; a business opportunity must itself be sound, with good potential for growth. But there's no doubt that the plan helped us to deliver our message clearly and concisely, and gave a crisp, professional first impression – and that undoubtedly accelerated the process of raising funds.

Later in the life of this business the tables turned and we ourselves became the investor. I was charged with looking at investment opportunities beyond the everyday scope of stocks and bonds. This meant that a whole range of enterprises presented deals to us – from start-up businesses looking for that first crucial injection of cash, all the way up to large multi-billion-dollar, publicly listed corporations.

One thing I learned was that the starting point of any sensible and serious dialogue was, without fail, always the same: 'Send us the details in writing' – and that meant their business plan. During the years that I spent in this role I saw many hundreds of business plans – most of which ended up in the bin. Many plans comprised pages and pages of irrelevant detail and, more often than not, I would only skim-read them in a desperate attempt to find the important points. Most failed to raise the money they needed, but some won their investment and were spectacularly successful.

One example of such a success was a blueberry farm in Uruguay. In this case, the management team predicted an imminent jump in global food prices, and wanted to expand into more general agriculture in the country. They raised more than eighty million dollars in just three months. Their success was based on the same foundation established by all of the businesses I saw that raised investment: this included a business plan with a consistent structure and presentation. The similarities shared by the successful plans suggested that this wasn't a matter of chance. I learned a great deal from observing how effective their fixed format was and experience taught me that all businesses – whatever their size, whatever sector they occupied – could use business plans that follow a consistent, generic structure.

Today I have come full circle – once again I'm starting a new venture. It needed an initial investment of several hundred thousand pounds. I wrote the plan in a few days, and had the terms of business agreed with an investor just a few weeks later. If you get your business plan right and know who to send it to, things can happen incredibly quickly.

My experience of working with hundreds of business plans – both as an entrepreneur desperately looking for cash, and then later as a financier – has equipped me to outline the most effective way of writing and presenting a business plan. In this book I will show you the simple rules and principles for writing a successful, professional business plan.

Putting it all together

Business Plans That Get Investment shows you an approach that is based on real-world, practical experience rather than theory. Follow this formula and you will be on your first step to getting your investment.

Writing a professional business plan does not require years of expensive education or training. It is not some 'dark art' that is known only to a select few. Anyone can do it: and all it needs is a little knowhow. The 'one size fits all' structure outlined in this book is quick and easy to apply, and is highly effective. It is suitable for any type of business and relevant for any size of investment. If you follow this structure it will save you a great deal of time and frustration, and free you to get on with what you really want to be doing: securing your investment and growing your business.

CHAPTER 2. FORMAT

I hope I have made it clear what a business plan is and why you need one. But before we start work on the actual structure and content of your business plan, it is important to discuss its format. By 'format' I mean the design, layout and media you use to present it. This may not seem like a particularly important issue to you but in fact it is crucial. Format can make the difference between whether an investor considers your business a serious proposition or dismisses it out of hand.

If you adhere to the formatting suggestions in this chapter, your plan will appear professional and serious, giving you a much-improved chance of creating a good first impression with any investor.

For your convenience, a template of what I regard as a model business plan is available to download from the website that accompanies this book, at www.businessplansthatgetinvestment.com. The template already conforms to the formatting points outlined in this chapter with the style, fonts, colours, and so on all prepared and set up for you.

Send the right signals

Getting the format of your plan right is more important than it may seem at first glance. No matter how much time, money or passion you have invested in your business idea, all of it can easily be wasted by sloppy or amateurish presentation. A properly formatted business plan that is visually consistent and professional in appearance sends a strong message of competence to a potential investor, and makes the content far easier for them to read. Good formatting is not particularly difficult – and thus there is no excuse not to ensure that your plan looks as impressive as possible.

Media / software required

Before considering the various design elements of your plan's format, you must decide on the type of media and software that you will use to write the plan. First of all – at the risk of stating the obvious – your plan must be prepared in a digital format. Investors expect this and it means that you can easily edit your plan as your business progresses, and when facts and information change. It is not an option to write your plan by hand and submit a photocopy!

At this point, most people will naturally think that a word-processing program such as Microsoft Word is the best place to start. After all, you are going to write your plan, so why not use a program designed to help you write? Do not make this mistake. A word-processing program will only encourage you to create more content and write more text. This should be avoided. Your business plan should be a written form of an 'elevator pitch', where the aim is to get your message across as quickly and clearly as possible.

A presentation software program is a far better option. The most commonly used is Microsoft PowerPoint, though other options include the free presentation programs from openoffice.org or Google. However, I recommend PowerPoint, as its functionality is very good and it is very straightforward to use once you've got the hang of it. And remember: I have prepared a template for you already.

You need to think of your business plan as a presentation that you must give in front of an audience. It is never a good idea to give a presentation that consists entirely of you reading from a prepared script. A business plan must therefore be presented as a series of slides that contain key points. A presentation program like PowerPoint is designed specifically to create just this type of format. By 'slides', I mean the types of pages that you will often see in a presentation, on which text can be placed freely in any position. This is different to the layout of a book, for example, where text positioning is more sequential, linear and formulaic.

In your plan, successive slides should have content that naturally flows from one slide to the next. It's useful to think of what is required here as something like telling a story. We'll explore this 'story flow' further a little later; but a slide-based approach helps to create a sequential flow, with each page covering a separate topic, and an overall effect of narrative development.

Learn to love bullet points

The use of bullet points will help with the presentation of your content on each slide. Bullet points are a key tool and make your plan easy to digest by breaking up the monotony of reading free-flowing text. They force you to work with shorter sentences and break your language into simple and quickly assimilated chunks. They encourage the use of short, direct sentences that help you to distil and focus your own thoughts, and thus to eliminate waffle. This enables you to get your message across to the investor more quickly and efficiently. Bullet points are fundamental to the success of your business plan.

Aim for a maximum of six bullet points per page, unless it is absolutely essential to use more. Take a look at the example at the end of this chapter. Ignore its contents for now; just look at how the bullet points break the content into easily readable sentences.

Be consistent

Consistency is very important throughout your plan. By 'consistency', I mean that the format and layout should be exactly the same from one slide to the next. Titles should be positioned in exactly the same place, and colours should be the same throughout – as should the use of typefaces, line-spacing, bullet point positioning, and so on.

Stylistic consistency is an area often overlooked. It is hard to overemphasise the degree to which inconsistency creates a poor impression. As an investor, a lack of consistency always puts me off, as it shows poor attention to detail.

The key elements to a good format

The numbered points below refer to the various elements you need to consider when putting together the format of your slides. You can see examples that comprise these elements at the end of this chapter.

1. **Main title page** – Always ensure that you have a title page that states the name of the business and the fact that it is a business plan. Think of it as analogous to the cover of a book. Include the date of the plan.
2. **Page titles** – Each slide must have its own title. Never, under any circumstances, leave a page without a title. The reader must

always have a reference point to the content that they are reading, and the title provides this.

3. **Dividers** – Insert a divider at the top of the page. This cleanly separates the content from the title.
4. **Page numbers** – Each page should be numbered. Place the numbers at the bottom right or bottom centre of the page.
5. **Logo / branding** – Any branding should remain discreet, and should not detract from the substantive content. I suggest that brand images are inserted above the upper divider line, to the right of the page.
6. **Line-spacing** – Keep plenty of space between lines so that the content remains easily legible.
7. **Font** – I use 'Arial' or 'Arial Narrow' in any plans I write. 'Verdana' is also good and was designed to be read on screen. Stick to one single font throughout the plan. On no account should 'comic' or decorative fonts be used – it looks unprofessional. Do not use 'Times New Roman' – it looks dated. Try to avoid excessive underlining and bold for emphasis.
8. **Font colour** – Use black or dark grey text. It may sound dull, but these are easier to read than other colours. Furthermore, colours such as blue and green can be lost or rendered illegible in a printout. Avoid red – it is hard to read and is associated with error messages.
9. **Background colour** – Always keep the background of your slides white. It looks professional and avoids the printing problems that can occur with a coloured background.
10. **Other colours** – For other elements in the plan, such as image titles, dividing lines, and so on, aim to keep the colour consistent with that of any branding you may have. For example, if your brand is blue, make any other associated colours blue, where possible.
11. **Images, charts and diagrams** – A picture can indeed paint a thousand words, so use them where they are relevant. Do not use clip art – it always looks amateurish.

Avoid spelling mistakes

There isn't much to say on this. Once you have written and completed the content of your business plan, check it for spelling mistakes. Then check it again. And then again. And then get someone else to check it!

There is no excuse for spelling mistakes. Poor spelling is sloppy and shows a lack of attention to detail.

Likewise, make sure that your grammar is correct. For example, I often see the misuse of apostrophes in business plans. People seem to add them when they are not needed or omit them where they are necessary.

Sometimes your grammar may be deliberately incorrect, especially in terms of structuring a sentence. In your plan, you will be making use of short, sharp statements. A grammatically correct sentence, full of articles and pronouns, may not be appropriate. Deliberate grammatical errors through the shortening of sentences are fine and are often expected in a business plan. For example, the following sentence:

Capital Technology Software is used by more than 2, 500 clients

may become:

Capital Technology >2, 500 clients

Convert to PDF

Once you have completed your plan and filled it with the content we are about to cover in this book, you will need to convert the finished product from PowerPoint into PDF format.

There are two reasons for this. Firstly, using a PDF format tends to look more professional. Secondly, PowerPoint has gone through many different versions over the years, and this can sometimes cause some compatibility problems between different users. The last thing you want is for a potential investor to receive your business plan by email and then be unable to open the document or see it with corrupted formatting.

You can easily convert your PowerPoint business plan into a PDF document by using one of many free conversion websites. I generally use www.freepdfconvert.com. It is very straightforward, and does not corrupt your design or formatting in any way. Alternatively, and easier still, later versions of PowerPoint give you the ability to 'save as' a PDF.

Example

Fig. 1 on the page opposite shows an example title page of a business plan.

Fig. 2 shows an example slide from the same business plan as the title page shown previously. Ignore the contents of the page for now, just note the formatting.

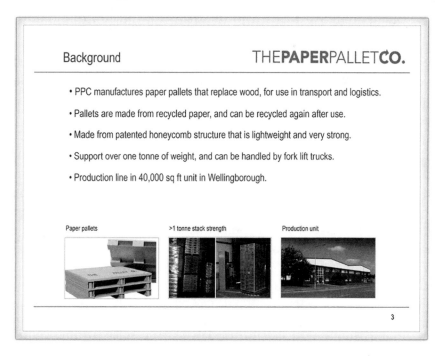

CHAPTER 3. STRUCTURE

Now we get down to business. Structure is the single most important thing when it comes to writing your plan. You ignore it at your peril. It is very simple: if you get the structure wrong then your plan won't work. That's the bad news. The good news is that the structure is possibly one of the easiest parts of your plan to get right, if you have the knowhow.

Indeed, I'd go as far as to say that if you get the structure of your plan right you have done 80 per cent of the hard work – the rest is just filling in the gaps with detail!

I still shake my head in disbelief when I think back to how, all those years ago, I struggled and fretted and agonised about writing my first business plan. If I had just understood how to structure my plan, and what elements to include within the resulting framework, life would have been so much easier. My main problem was that I was not aware of what investors needed to see in the plan, and so my structure was a mess. I did not include sections that I should have realised were essential – and some of the sections that I did include were, in fact, superfluous. As I did not get the structure right, my plan did not really make sense and was not coherent. It was not as concise as it should have been, and there was a lot of irrelevant content.

What is the 'structure'?

What do I mean when I refer to the 'structure' of a business plan? In effect, I am simply referring to the correct presentation and sequencing of issues that a potential investor will expect you to address. This sequence ensures that your plan follows a logical path, with each part following on naturally from the previous one. A good structure makes it easy for the reader to follow your reasoning and understand your business – what it is, why it will work, and, most importantly, why it represents an attractive investment opportunity.

It's not so different to writing a story. You don't write 'Once upon a time…' at the end or the middle of a story. Likewise, in a business plan you don't include the section called 'Executive Summary' at the end, or the section called 'Exit' at the beginning.

Correct title sequence

The titles of your slides and the order that you place them in should correspond to the issues you must cover in your business plan. Mapping out your structure with correct and relevant titles on each of your slides is a crucial step, as it enables the reader to understand easily what each slide in the plan relates to. To clarify what I mean, the chapter in your business plan that explains the opportunity that your business addresses will have the title 'Opportunity'. Likewise, the chapter that addresses the competition that your business faces will have the title 'Competition'.

Almost all of the successful plans that I have seen essentially follow the same structure. The sequence of pages in your plan, and the corresponding titles, should be as follows:

1. **Executive Summary** – An overview of what is to come in the plan. Think of it as an introduction.
2. **Opportunity** – Why your business exists. In effect, what problem or gap in the market your business addresses.
3. **Background** – What it is that your business makes or does.
4. **USP** – USP stands for 'Unique Selling Point'. This relates to what it is that makes your business special and different from others.
5. **Progress** – What progress you have made with developing your business and its current position, including any successes you have had to date.
6. **The Market** – The identity and characteristics of your customers.
7. **Route to Market** – How you plan to access and sell to your potential customers.
8. **Competition** – Who else does what you do, or something similar.
9. **Management** – Who runs the business, and what is their experience and knowledge in the sector.
10. **Business Model** – How the business makes money. It explains the cost of manufacture of the product, or provision of the service, through to the proceeds from actual sales.

11. **Financials** – Current and future sales, costs, and profits.
12. **Investment** – How much investment you are asking for, and what you plan to do with it.
13. **Exit** – How an investor will get their money back from their investment and generate an additional return.
14. **Conclusion** – A brief synopsis of the plan. Similar to the Executive Summary, but highlighting the most favourable points in the plan, so that it finishes on a 'high note'.

The structure works for any business

The vast majority of businesses will need a plan that conforms to this single template – and this holds true for the structure more than any other aspect of the plan. Do not stray from this structure unless you are certain that you have a good reason for doing so.

For example, some businesses may have very specific attributes that require an extra section or two. Or you might need more than one page to effectively emphasise an important aspect of your business. That's fine as long as it is really necessary. If so, you should use the same title, but add '(continued)' after it. For example, the slide called 'Management' may be followed by another slide entitled 'Management (continued)'. It is far better to do this than to try to jam too much information into a single slide, which will only end up looking cluttered and messy. But I would recommend avoiding the repetition of a slide title unless it is absolutely necessary for you to get your message across.

By preparing a set of titled slides, you have in effect created the structure you need for an effective business plan. A template called 'Structure' is available to download from the website that accompanies this book (www.businessplansthatgetinvestment.com). It uses my recommended structure, prepared in a fully formatted design.

Correct structure gives you direction

An advantage of getting your structure right at the outset is that it maps out the content that is required for each of the relevant pages of your plan. In effect, it gives you a roadmap as to where you should be going, and what you should be saying when. I guarantee that it will save you endless hours of work, allow you to produce relevant content quickly and thus prepare an effective plan.

It is no different to writing a novel. You wouldn't expect to blindly start scribbling away on a new thriller without having a vision as to what the story will be, including its essential twists and turns. A business plan must be approached in the same way.

In short, structure is crucial. Fortunately, it is easy to get right once you know how. Best of all, when you have the structure in place, you know you have done the hardest part of creating your business plan. You will have a guide as to what the content should be on each page and thereby a roadmap to completion.

PART 2

WRITING THE PLAN

CHAPTER 4. APPLICATION

The structure and format of your business plan should now be clear. Your fourteen-page PowerPoint presentation is prepared, with a separate title on each page. The next step is to add the relevant content to each page. To help you with this process, the next fourteen chapters will cover the fourteen structure titles that were outlined in the previous chapter. Each chapter will explain what content you should be writing for that page in the plan and also what information you need to provide, and how to obtain it. Worked examples will be provided throughout to help you along.

The worked examples are all based on actual businesses. Some of these examples are taken from real business plans and others have been tailored to help emphasise a point. Some names, facts or figures may have been changed where it might be commercially sensitive. All of the examples shown in this book are available to download as PowerPoint templates from the website.

CHAPTER 5. EXECUTIVE SUMMARY

After the main title page, your plan should start with a page entitled 'Executive Summary'. The aim of this page is to highlight the key points of your entire business plan in several bullet points. Think of it as an introduction, explaining what your plan is all about. In effect, this page is a snapshot of what you are going to say in the rest of the document. Your reader should be able to understand the key elements of your business plan from a two-minute skim-read. If you arouse their interest here, they are far more likely to read on.

However, the Executive Summary is best written once all of the other chapters are finished. Those completed chapters will guide you on what to write in the Executive Summary, saving you time and effort. So we will return to this chapter later, once we have worked through all of the other chapters in the plan.

So, for now, simply create a page with the necessary formatting and with the title of 'Executive Summary', and leave the rest of the slide blank.

CHAPTER 6. OPPORTUNITY

The purpose of the second page in your plan is to set the scene. What you are doing in this chapter is demonstrating to the investor what unmet need your product or service addresses. If your business can solve a problem and make life easier for your customers it has a good chance of succeeding. At this point in the plan you only need to explain the problem that your business addresses, not what your business actually does – that comes later. In explaining the problem, you are demonstrating the business opportunity.

Why do opportunities arise?

Business opportunities can stem from a variety of circumstances, some of which I have listed below. Business opportunities may occur because

- a successful business exists elsewhere in the world but does not yet exist in your home country;
- changes in technology or science allow for a more effective resolution of an existing issue;
- new technology or other innovation creates a new problem that did not previously exist;
- consumer habits or demographics change, creating new opportunities – for example, a trend towards organic, healthier food among the Western middle classes.

The list could clearly be extended significantly – but it should give you a sense of what I mean.

Explain the opportunity

Irrespective of the opportunity, you must resist the temptation to explain here what your business actually does. Likewise, avoid areas such as the scale of the opportunity, who your competition is, and so on. All of that comes later in the plan. At this stage you must stick to the discipline of explaining effectively what opportunity it exploits – just as stories begin traditionally by setting the scene before the action begins.

Incidentally, this is not the place to include your personal reasons for starting a business. There's no need to tell the investor that you want to be your own boss, you want to get rich, and so on. You must focus on the objective commercial evidence for the business opportunity that you have identified. All subjective and personal feelings should be left out of your plan.

That does not mean that you shouldn't be passionate about what you are doing, especially when you come to present your plan to investors face-to-face. Passion is important, and investors like to see that an entrepreneur is personally committed to what they are doing. At this stage in the plan, though, your personal motivations and subjective views and feelings are not relevant. Their inclusion would only make you look unprofessional.

Examples of opportunities

To illustrate how you should describe an opportunity, I will draw on two real examples that I have seen raise funding.

Example 1: Credit card covers

'Chip and pin' payment technology is in every shop and retail outlet in the UK. If you want to pay for your purchases with a debit or credit card, you must take your card out, insert it into a card reader, wait a few seconds for recognition, enter your pin code, and then wait a few seconds more for authorisation. However, this somewhat manual process is fast becoming redundant. Technological advances mean that all we have to do when we want to pay for something is swipe our card, or indeed our phone in some cases, in the general proximity of a reader. No pin codes and no fiddling around to insert cards – just a quick swipe. It works much like the Oyster card readers currently in use on the London transport network.

This innovation dramatically speeds up the payment process for an individual consumer, which in turn translates to an increase in sales for the retailer. Indeed, I recall reading research that, for higher volume retailers (such as supermarkets), the speeding up of the payment process by just 5 seconds equates to an increase of 1.7 per cent in overall sales – a significant improvement.

But there is a catch to this wonderful new technology. Theoretically there is little to stop a criminal from getting within scanning distance of you and 'swiping' your card without your knowledge, using a mobile card reader.

This is clearly a problem, presenting an opportunity for a product or technology to address it. I recently saw a new business that was doing just that.

The business owners had created a slim payment card carrier that was made of a material that blocks all wireless communication to and from cards within. This immediately solved the problem of criminals accessing the card data: while your cards are in the protective case, they are impossible to 'swipe' wirelessly. When you want to use a card, you press an eject button, and a small section of the card that carries the wireless 'aerial' pops out and is exposed. You can now 'contactlessly' swipe the card at the point of sale, and then just press it back into its case. A simple but innovative solution to a security problem.

So how should you present this opportunity in a business plan? As explained in Chapter 3, you should articulate the opportunity in a few clear bullet point statements. Indeed, by the time you finish this book, you will be sick of reading this advice. However, after structure, bullet points are your most important tool in writing a business plan!

Fig. 3 overleaf shows how your bullet points would read for this example. I have added images that illustrate how contactless payment differs from chip-and-pin payment, and also an image that shows a criminal contactlessly 'swiping' a card in someone's bag or wallet. These images help to illustrate the problem that gives rise to the business opportunity.

- Debit/Credit card payments in shops currently use 'chip and pin' technology.
- 'Contactless' card readers rapidly replacing 'chip and pin'.
- By 2017, estimated 83% of all UK retail outlets operate contactless payments.
- Widespread concern around 'wireless' crime, and the ability for criminals to 'contactlessly swipe' cards with ease.

Traditional Chip and Pin

Contactless Payment

Contactless Theft

2

Example 2: Online repeat prescriptions

My second example is based on a business that a good friend of mine started a decade or so ago. They were the first in the UK to offer an online facility for requesting repeat medical prescriptions, and he set the precedent for a process that has now become commonplace.

Until this point, patients would have to make an appointment to see their family doctor, then visit the surgery in person to obtain the doctor's signature, and finally go to the pharmacy to collect their medicine – a time-consuming and frustrating process, to say the least. The reason for this was that UK health regulations stipulated that a repeat prescription had to be approved by a qualified medical practitioner.

My friend's business overcame this regulatory hurdle by creating a website where users could enter the relevant details in order to apply for their repeat prescription. A team of doctors would then review the details online and, where appropriate, approve the prescription application. The medicine would then be sent directly to the patient's home.

The idea was a great success. Within just three years of launching the service, the business was sold to one of the UK's largest pharmacy chains for a substantial sum of money. This is a great example of how new technology can make a process better and more efficient, and how that technology was used to overcome a regulatory hurdle, thereby creating a great business opportunity.

Had I written the business plan for my friend, the opportunity slide would have taken the following form, shown in **Fig. 4**. Note that the opportunity in this example is no longer valid as it has been overtaken by events, with online repeat prescriptions now commonplace.

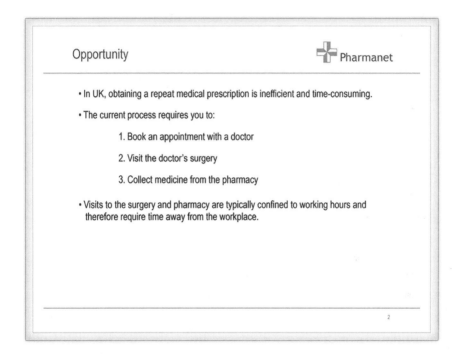

Address a problem or need

A word of warning here. If you cannot demonstrate the opportunity that your business takes advantage of, and thus why there would be demand for your product or service, then you need to think very carefully about whether it is a viable business in the first place. A large number of businesses fail simply because, although they have identified an innovative and creative idea, they do not really make anyone's life better or more efficient, and therefore fail to find a market in the real world.

The aim of the 'opportunity page' is that the reader should understand the specific problem that your business addresses. In effect, you are demonstrating why there will be demand for what it is that your business offers. If you are able to convey this successfully, an investor will be able to grasp the context that makes your business an attractive commercial opportunity.

Opportunity summary:

- Demonstrate the problem or issue that your business addresses. This is your opportunity.
- Focus solely on making clear what the opportunity is. Do not explain yet what your business does.
- Do not attempt to quantify the opportunity – that comes later.
- Use images, if they are relevant and if they can illustrate the nature of the opportunity.
- Remember: by explaining the opportunity you are showing why there is, or will be, demand for your product or service.

CHAPTER 7. BACKGROUND

The aim of this part of your plan is to outline what it is that your business does. This sounds simple enough and if your business manufactures a single product then it should be straightforward. However, even if your business is not easily encapsulated, you must still be very clear about what it is that you offer. I have seen countless presentations that have left me scratching my head, questioning what the actual business is – a situation that will never result in investment. This is a mistake to be avoided at all costs.

Introduce what your business does

The first step is to describe your business in one or two sentences, summarising it in your first bullet point. This first statement acts as a sort of mini 'introduction' to your business and to the explanation that is to follow. This sounds easy enough but in fact it can prove quite tricky to condense the necessary information into a concise sentence – especially when you have probably spent months or even years immersed in your idea. Don't worry if you have a lot more to say about the detail of your product as there will be ample opportunity to elaborate later.

Businesses typically fall into one of two categories, offering either a product or a service. Let's take a real, product-based example from my own experience. The business was called Pembroke Interactive and it produced CD-ROMs about famous tourist attractions and heritage sites. Having seen the phenomenal success of a French business that was doing something similar in the heritage sector, I decided to replicate their business model for the UK.

CD-ROMs were a popular product in the 1990s – a bit like an e-book but with text, images and video packaged onto a compact disc that could be viewed on a computer. Since then, they have been superseded by the internet, which now has much faster connection speeds and makes much more content (that would have otherwise been on a CD-ROM) freely available. A CD-ROM business might seem like a rather dated example but, because of the nature of the business and the simplicity of the product, it works as an excellent example throughout the book and emphasises the timeless effectiveness of the business plan structure I have laid out for you.

Going back to Pembroke Interactive as a product-based business, the first bullet point on the slide in the business plan read something like this:

- Pembroke Interactive Ltd produces CD-ROMs specialising in the heritage sector.

Now let's take a look at a service business. A friend of mine runs an organic food wholesaler. This means that he sells organic fruit and vegetables to various restaurants and food retailers throughout London. The first bullet point on the slide of his plan reads:

- Organic Republic (OR) is an organic food wholesaler in London.

Just to be clear, I use 'service business' to refer to a business that does not produce a tangible product, but rather offers a 'service' in the sense of providing expertise, or facilitating another business. For example, a law firm is a service business because it sells specific expertise to a client. Likewise, a stockbroker is a service business because it facilitates the buying and selling of shares.

More detail

Once you have the first sentence down to a pithy one-liner, you should aim to use the next bullet point statements on the page to provide more detail about what your business does.

In the case of the CD-ROM business, these would be the following bullet points:

- Pembroke Interactive Ltd produces CD-ROMs, specialising in the heritage sector.

- Each CD-ROM production focuses on a world-famous heritage / historic site. Examples include *HMS Victory*, the world's most visited warship, and the British Museum, with its >1m visitors per year.
- The CD-ROMs comprise extensive written, photographic and multimedia content.

And there you have it: the CD-ROM business explained in three concise bullet points.

At this point you may insist that your business is so complex that it is impossible to explain it in three or four concise statements. I suspect that is not the case. Any business can be described in broad, simple terms; if you cannot do so, you are over-complicating things.

For example, let's take what is probably one of the most complex scientific pieces of hardware ever built, the Large Hadron Collider. I confess that I don't know exactly what it does but I do know that, no matter how complicated it is, it can be described concisely. To prove my point, this is the first sentence from its Wikipedia page:

'The Large Hadron Collider (LHC) is the world's largest and highest-energy particle accelerator.'

This single sentence doesn't tell us what exactly a particle accelerator is, how it works, or what purpose it serves but it does give us a description that acts as a jumping-off point for exploring further detail.

Another potential problem is that your business may offer several different products and / or services, and incorporate a number of revenue streams.

Let's return to my friend's organic food wholesale business. We already know that he sells organic fruit and vegetables to restaurants and food retailers throughout London; but that is not all his business does. Because he has vans making deliveries throughout central London every day, he also uses his business's excess space in the vans to offer a logistics service to other food wholesalers who are not in natural competition with him. His logic is that, if he has spare space in his vans when making his deliveries, why not offer a delivery service to other businesses that need to make deliveries in central London? This creates additional revenue for him on journeys and deliveries that he would otherwise be making anyway, and it makes sound commercial sense.

This kind of 'business within a business' naturally makes the overarching business harder to condense into just a few sentences when you are explaining what it does – but that should still be the aim. For example, the two revenue streams of the organic food wholesaler can be easily explained:

- Organic Republic is an organic food wholesaler, based in London.
- It offers central London logistics and delivery services to other wholesalers based on existing infrastructure.

As I have mentioned, do not concern yourself at this stage with the details of who you sell to, how much money you make, your key selling points, your achievements, and so on. Likewise, there is no need to talk about who owns the business, how many employees it has, how much it sells, and so on. All of this will come later in the plan. Your sole objective on this page of your business plan is to explain to the reader what it is that your business does.

Not summarising will mean no investment

If your business interests are so diverse and unrelated that it is impossible to explain your business in a few simple, summary statements, I strongly recommend that you stop and think about precisely what it is you are doing and work out for what specific purpose you are going to use the investment you are seeking. Investors hate a lack of focus and they are right to take this approach. Lack of focus is fatal and can quickly render an opportunity dead in the water.

A picture paints a thousand words

Images can be hugely helpful in explaining what your business does. If it relates to a product, show pictures of the product and ideally pictures of it in use. This will immediately convey what it is that you do, bringing your explanation to life. In the case of Organic Republic it makes sense to show pictures of the vegetable produce, of the warehouse, and so on. This helps to show that it is a real and tangible business and not just an idea. **Fig. 5** on the following page demonstrates the use of images.

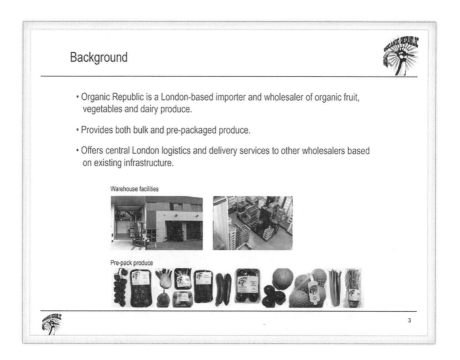

Background

- Organic Republic is a London-based importer and wholesaler of organic fruit, vegetables and dairy produce.

- Provides both bulk and pre-packaged produce.

- Offers central London logistics and delivery services to other wholesalers based on existing infrastructure.

Warehouse facilities

Pre-pack produce

3

Further examples

The next example is from the business plan for a product called 'Wavecave'. Travelling and surfing go hand in hand, as surfers invariably move from one place to the next in search of suitable waves. Inevitably they end up carrying a lot of equipment, which can be inconvenient. A clear opportunity presents itself and is ideal for inclusion on the second slide of a perfect business plan. The three big pieces of kit that surfers have to carry around are a surfboard, a tent, and a sleeping mat. The surfboards are stored in protective bags to prevent dents and scratches in transport.

In a 'eureka moment', the business owners came up with the 'Wavecave' – a protective surfboard bag that folds out to become a tent with a built-in sleeping mat. It means that you only need to carry one piece of gear, rather than three. The Wavecave team entitled this slide in their business plan 'What is a Wavecave?' instead of 'Background', but the purpose of the page is the same. The layout works well and explains what the product is very clearly (**Fig. 6** – see overleaf).

Following on, the next example (**Fig. 7** – see page opposite) shows a plan for a business that is reclaiming an unused and uninhabited area of swampland adjacent to a fast-growing, major city in sub-Saharan Africa. The aim of the project was to employ local workers and businesses to reclaim the land with minimal environmental impact and to develop essential infrastructure in the surrounding area. This new land is then used to build residential and commercial properties on, as well as amenities such as shops, and local services. Take a look at the next example and see how much more the images bring to life the explanation of the business that I just gave.

Finally, for one more example, you can refer back to **Fig. 2** in the 'Format' chapter, earlier in the book, in Part One. The example relates to a fantastic business that makes the equivalent of wooden transport pallets from recycled paper. These paper pallets have a real and positive environmental impact – they are lighter than wooden ones and therefore save on fuel costs and also reduce deforestation.

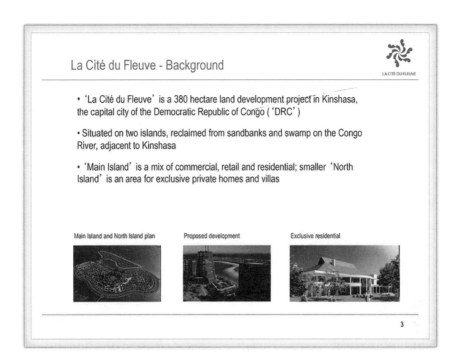

Background summary:

- Explain what your business does.
- Be clear and concise. Keep it to as few sentences as reasonably possible.
- There is no need for detail relating to how you make money, who you are, your current progress, etc. All of this will come later in the plan.
- Even if your business is complex or has multiple aspects, you must aim to keep the message concise. If you over-complicate things, you will lose your reader.
- Do not be afraid of using more than one slide to convey your message if your business is not a simple one and definitely requires it. This is better than crowding a page with too much information.
- Use images as much as you can: a picture speaks a thousand words. Images also keep things more interesting for the reader.

CHAPTER 8. USP

USP stands for 'unique selling point' and is a term used widely throughout the world's business schools and MBA classes. USP refers to the factor (or factors) that make your product or service special. It is the unique ingredient of your business that sets you apart from your competition, and opens up your particular path to success.

While it is true that not all businesses are unique, most new businesses will have something that differentiates them from their competition. This acts as a 'wedge' that can help them break into an existing market.

Be different

Let's take the example of a public relations (PR) firm. If I were to start a new PR firm – which would put me in what is already a very competitive, crowded sector – I would be keen to identify some means by which my business could distinguish itself from the thousands of other PR firms out there. Focusing on a specialised area is one way of achieving this, and thus creating a USP.

I asked a friend who owns a PR firm what her business's USP was. She explained that her company specialises exclusively in luxury family hotels, which makes it entirely unique in the UK. This focus on a specific niche means that she is far more likely to win business in this area. Her business has developed a clear advantage, even though the involvement of PR in the tourism sector is nothing new or unique in itself.

Intellectual property

What else can make a business unique? Well, intellectual property is another example, invariably in the form of a new product or process.

Investors love it if you have a unique idea and have been able to protect it with patents.

A patent is an exclusive right, granted to anyone who invents any new, useful, and non-obvious process or product. A patent must protect an actual physical product or process; it cannot apply simply to an idea. For example, you cannot patent the idea of a time machine; but if you happen to invent one, you can patent the process and mechanism by which it functions. Once you have been granted the patent by the relevant authorities, you have exclusive rights so that the process or product may not be legally copied within the geographical territory specified by the patent.

Be aware that patents can be extremely expensive, especially when they have global reach. There are many layers of fees associated with obtaining and maintaining a patent, and they quickly mount up. Over the years, you should expect patents to cost tens of thousands of pounds and possibly hundreds of thousands.

The good news is the legal concept of 'patent pending'. This refers to a period, typically a couple of years, during which your patent submission is reviewed and remains open to scrutiny. Your invention is still protected, and cannot be legally copied if the patent is eventually approved. During this period the costs tend to be much lower, which gives you an opportunity to 'test the water' and gauge whether your product or idea is viable without burning through too much money in fees. Investors understand the merits of this approach, so make sure that you highlight any patent pending in your business plan.

Sadly, you should expect the competition to copy you even if you do have a watertight patent in place. If it is a good product, they certainly will. This insight is a result of bitter experience on my part, rather than a tendency towards cynicism. A patent is thus only worth what you are willing and able to pay to protect it once you have secured it.

Nevertheless, if you are thinking big, patents can be the difference between making millions or going bankrupt. Look at James Dyson, the billionaire inventor of the bagless vacuum cleaner. Without secure patents in place, and their successful legal protection against some big, multinational names, his business might not even exist today.

Patents are also helpful when you come to sell your business. Indeed, it may even be the rights to your intellectual property that a buyer is specifically interested in.

Trademarks and copyright are other ways of protecting intellectual property. They tend to be conceptually more straightforward, and generally relate to the protection of original work such as music, writing or artwork, usually for a limited period. If I write something, you cannot reproduce it without my permission. Trademarks are similar, but they relate to protecting a brand name or logo design.

First-mover advantage

'First-mover advantage' is another significant type of USP. In simple terms, this means that you are the first, or more realistically among the first, to bring a new product or service to market. This gives you a clear head start over any potential competitors who might be planning to enter the same space, or who are drawn into an area by your initial first blush of success.

We all understand intuitively that it is harder to muscle in on any competitive activity that is already well established, rather than being the first on the scene. This concept is often referred to as a 'barrier to entry' and extends beyond just being the first-mover; it applies to any competitive business situation whereby it is hard for a new entrant in your market to get a foothold.

As it happens, I don't entirely share the widely held view that to be the first is always best. First-mover advantage is great, but it does mean that you have to educate your market on the nature and benefits of your product or service, and that can be expensive. Moreover, the very fact of being the first to do something means that the concept behind it is commercially untested, and may fail to bear fruit. In other words, there are such things as first-mover disadvantages!

But despite these apparent challenges, some of the world's most successful businesses were among the first movers in their sector, especially in areas of new technology – most obviously Apple, Facebook, Google, and so on.

First-mover advantage can be a very powerful USP, and it should always be included in your plan if applicable.

Do it better

This raises the issue of another type of USP: to put it bluntly – simply doing something better than everyone else. I recall a conversation

I had with the founder of a large London residential estate agency, which he eventually sold for several hundred million pounds. He described many ways in which his company did things better, albeit within an established, indeed traditional, business sector. For example, they offered property viewings after working hours. It seems obvious: people are busy at work and don't have time to view a property during the day, so why on earth wouldn't you offer the service of late viewings?

'What makes a USP?' recap

There are many factors that might offer up that magic USP. To summarise, here are a few that spring to mind:

- new product innovation, patent protected
- first-mover advantage through innovation
- first-mover advantage in your region – e.g. you may replicate a product or service that exists elsewhere in the world but not in your country
- specialisation in a specific area or niche within an existing sector
- improvement on an existing product or service
- cheaper / more cost-effective solution than an existing offering
- exceptional management team and deep relationships in an industry that will inevitably generate business
- exclusive arrangements that 'block' others from competing with you – a good example of a 'barrier to entry'

This list is in no way exhaustive, and its contents are certainly not mutually exclusive; you can have more than one USP!

Presentation

The next issue is how to present your USPs in your business plan. As always, you need to follow the clear bullet point format. Let's take a look at an example for an imaginary product. In the plan, the bullet point statements would be something like this:

- Acmeplug is a new product; nothing comparable exists to date
- Patent pending; filed July 2010

- Patent covering Europe, North America, Japan and Australasia
- Genuine first-mover advantage
- Competitive lead time of at least 18 months

The first of these points is perfectly clear: this is a new product. The second statement is also very clear. Indeed, if you have any kind of patent protection, it is essential that you state this fact clearly.

It is worth stating when your patents were filed, when they were approved and for which territories they are applicable. The timing of filings and awards can be important, as patents are finite; this information will help to build a picture of how much value there is in your business. Clearly, if a patent is set to expire in two years, then the business is less valuable than if it were set to expire in twenty years. If you don't include this type of information, any interested investor will certainly request it at some point.

The penultimate point states that, due to your innovative product or service, you have clear first-mover advantage. The final point indicates how long it would consequently take a competitor to enter this market from a standing start – i.e. the time it would take a competitor to bring an idea from concept through to a money-generating product or service.

Take this type of bullet point format and apply it to your own business. Don't worry if you don't have any patents. Just think about what your USPs are, and use this page to demonstrate them. Don't be concerned if it seems simplistic – as ever, the more you can distil what you are saying into simple points, the more effectively it will communicate your message.

Let's consider the CD-ROM business again. How would I present the USP page? CD-ROMs were not an original concept, and the process was certainly not patentable. **Fig. 8** on the page opposite clearly highlights why Pembroke Interactive has an advantage over others – despite the fact that the creation of heritage CD-ROMs was nothing new. Indeed, it was already an established business model: in the early 1990s a business called Montparnasse Multimedia sold over 1 million copies of its Louvre Museum CD-ROM in France! The important point in relation to the USP is that Pembroke Interactive was the first to focus on this specific area in the UK.

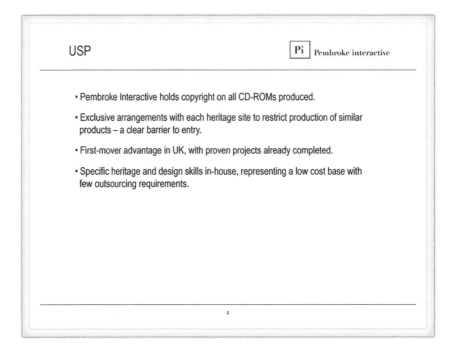

USP

Pi Pembroke interactive

- Pembroke Interactive holds copyright on all CD-ROMs produced.

- Exclusive arrangements with each heritage site to restrict production of similar products – a clear barrier to entry.

- First-mover advantage in UK, with proven projects already completed.

- Specific heritage and design skills in-house, representing a low cost base with few outsourcing requirements.

4

USP summary:

- Demonstrate your USPs – what makes you better, different or new.
- Highlight any intellectual property held by the business.
- Show expertise and speciality in a specific sector niche.
- The fact that a product or service is offered elsewhere does not mean that you cannot do it better. It is perfectly plausible to have a USP in an already crowded market.
- Outline all of your USPs, not just the biggest and best. USPs are not mutually exclusive, and you can have more than one.

CHAPTER 9. PROGRESS

By this point in your business plan, your reader will understand the context that makes your business a sound idea ('Opportunity'), what it is that your business does ('Background'), and what makes it special or unique ('USP'). This next chapter in your plan explains what progress your business has made so far. It is really a snapshot of what your current situation is and what you have achieved to date. The reason for providing this information in your plan is to demonstrate 'proof of concept'.

Proof of concept

'Proof of concept' refers to firm evidence that a product or service is commercially viable, and thus likely to make money. All this really means is that you can demonstrate tangibly (prove) that your business idea (concept) has the potential to become a commercial reality. For example, if you have a business idea, until you generate any sales, that is all it is – an idea. But if you have an idea that is backed up by actual sales, even if they don't amount to much at the early stages, it still shows an investor that people are prepared to pay for what you are offering.

By demonstrating proof of concept, you are validating your business and demonstrating that it is credible. In effect, proof of concept shows that your business is something that is real and can make money, rather than just a pipe dream. Without proof of concept in some form, it is far harder to convince an investor of the commercial merits of your business. It can often make the difference between whether an investment is made or not. Indeed, I am often surprised by how many start-up entrepreneurs disregard this fact. They seem to think that a great idea is enough. Sadly, that is not the case.

Demonstrate progress

Personally, I like to call this chapter 'Progress' – though I have seen other perfectly good plans that call it 'Current Status' or, on a more upbeat note, 'Achievements'. All of these are acceptable and relate to the same thing, so you should choose something that suits your style and personality.

How do you demonstrate the progress that you have made so far, and what are the key elements to be included? If your business has achieved any objective milestones that demonstrate proof of concept, it is absolutely essential that you show them on this page of your plan.

Such milestones will include the following, in order of importance:

1. **Sales to date** – If you have sold any of your product or service, it is absolutely essential to show that here: it is without doubt the single most important milestone you can indicate. Quite simply, it is the best 'proof of concept' there is. A record of proven sales takes a lot of the risk and uncertainty out of the equation for an investor, and will increase their willingness to make an investment. It gives credence to your story and clearly demonstrates to investors that a market exists for your business. You can present this fact very easily in bullet point format. Don't dwell too much on detail for now – just stick to the essentials. For example:

   • Sales in 2011: £234K

2. **Prominent or industry-leading clients** – Closely linked to sales themselves is any relationship you have with well-known or industry-leading clients. If you have a prominent client – especially if it is a large, blue-chip corporation – it is something you absolutely must highlight. Investors love blue-chip companies as clients; they are unlikely to go bust, and so represent a reliable flow of business, and will have no trouble making payments when they are due.

   Equally, if you operate in a sector where a more generalist investor may not know the big companies that are specific to that area, and you have one or more of these names as clients, you should outline them and their prominence within the sector by specifying their market position and size.

   Even if your clients are not market leaders, but you have managed to gain a foothold based on relationships with several smaller clients, it is still important to mention this fact. Rather than simply listing them all, it is a better idea to make a statement mentioning how many clients you have.

Finally, if you have clients across different geographical regions or countries, you should say so. This will show an investor that your product or service has international appeal and is not just restricted to your domestic market. This demonstrates that there is scope for further growth internationally.

A few years back my Auntie Helen invented a new type of mop – I'll tell you more about it later. But for now, the bullet points on her plan that related to her clients looked something like this:

- Prominent UK brand clients including John Lewis and Lakeland
- Sold into >18 distributors globally, across N. America, Asia, Europe and Australasia

3. **Distributors and partnerships** – If you have developed any distribution arrangements you should say so in your plan (these are sometimes known as 'channel partnerships', but I'll go into more detail on this topic later). By 'distribution arrangements', I mean agreements whereby other businesses resell your product after buying it from you, or sell it on your behalf. Though this is perhaps less important than actual sales, it is still highly relevant – especially if the distributor concerned is a well-known name in the sector.

In the same way that you demonstrate that you have clients, you should also outline any relationships with distributors and sales agents. In the case of the CD-ROM business:

- Distributors include Gardners Books, the UK's largest book distributor
- Distribution arrangements in place for N. America region

The nature of the partnership may not be limited to distribution. For example, you may have an agreement with a firm to which you outsource business. This might relate not only to sales, but also to other elements of your business – for example, outsourced manufacturing, or a call centre. Any relationships you have with larger, more established businesses enhance the credibility of your own business. A well-established business is clearly able to pick and choose whom they do business with; if they have chosen to work with you, that reflects well on your business.

4. **Contracts and negotiations** – A little further down the food chain are contracts that you have in place, but that have not yet yielded any sales, or negotiations that are underway with potential clients or distributors.

   As an investor, a phrase that you will inevitably hear during business pitches is 'We are talking to ...'. This often means nothing, and investors will simply disregard it as naive optimism or name-dropping. Investors know that 'talks' and 'discussions' with clients frequently fail to result in deals that produce cold, hard cash.

   However, if your 'discussions' do have real substance to them, then they are worth mentioning – especially in the absence yet of any real sales! So what does 'real substance' mean? Well, it certainly doesn't mean that you have made a call to a prospective client, who has said that your proposal sounds interesting and they will get back to you. What it does mean includes, among other things:

   - several meetings having taken place, including communication with senior (board level) management;
   - terms in formal negotiation;
   - terms agreed, currently being drafted into a legal contract;
   - a formal sales order that has not yet been fulfilled.

5. **Endorsements and media coverage** – If your business has collected any relevant endorsements, accolades or awards, then you must enumerate them clearly at this point. Endorsements can come from a range of sources, many of which will be valid and relevant for inclusion on this page of your plan. They may cover:

   - Awards and prizes. Include who the award comes from.
   - Trade press, including industry-specific magazines, publications and internet sites and blogs.

- Wider press and media coverage. If you have been covered in a story by a well-known media name, such as the BBC or a leading newspaper, then make sure that you show this. It says to an investor that your business is distinctive enough to warrant airtime or page space. It also shows that you are capable of promoting yourself and able to push your story out to the wider world.

- Celebrity endorsements. If you have a formal agreement in place for a celebrity to endorse your business, you must say so. However, if you can point to informal endorsements, such as a celebrity using your product, you should highlight this as well. If you can attribute a useful quote to the celebrity directly, so much the better. This is particularly relevant for retail products. Clearly, if David Beckham says that a certain type of football boot is best, or Naomi Campbell expresses a preference for a lipstick brand, that will have a positive impact on sales. Indeed, such is the power of celebrity endorsement that you could probably swap the two products between these celebrities, and still see a positive effect!

If you are skilled, shrewd or lucky enough to win positive coverage, or endorsement from such organisations, it is a good idea to insert the logos of the relevant endorsing organisations at the bottom of the page of this chapter in your plan. This approach is common practice on many consumer websites, as it creates an impression of authenticity through an association with big-brand media names. The same is true for your plan: logos make the page visually striking and the reader will immediately recognise any well-known brands and associate them with your business. Likewise, the same can be said for celebrity endorsement and you might want to insert a picture of the celebrity with a reference to them and perhaps a quote about the product or service that you offer.

Example

Fig. 9 on the page opposite shows an example of the 'Progress' slide from the African land development business that was mentioned earlier in the book. Note how clearly it demonstrates relevant progress. The page highlights the fact that it is now making real money, and is thus a viable business proposition.

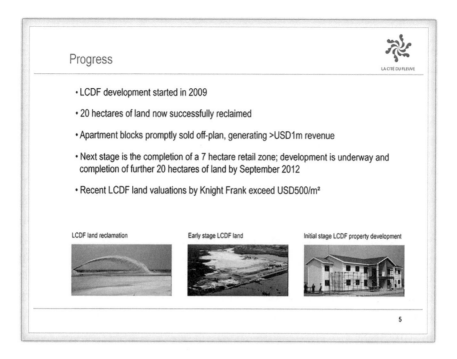

Progress summary:

- Demonstrate 'proof of concept', which is fundamental to any investment being made. Do not underestimate the value of this.
- Show any sales to date – this is crucial to your credibility.
- Highlight any brand name or industry-leading clients. The bigger the better!
- Show any distribution arrangements that are in place – especially with well-known names and industry leaders.
- Note any contracts or negotiations that are in progress but not yet completed.
- Be wary of the term 'We are in discussions with…'. You might look foolish if, when challenged, you are unable to provide any substance behind this sort of claim.
- Include any awards, accolades or endorsements that your business has received.
- Add logos or pictures of any well-known brands or public figures that you are dealing with, or from whom you have received endorsements.

CHAPTER 10. MARKET

The aim of this part of your business plan is to demonstrate two things to an investor: firstly, who your client base is, and secondly, that the sector in which your business operates has the size and growth potential for your business to succeed. This potential client base and the associated business sector is often referred to as your 'market'. By demonstrating the size and growth potential of this client base, you are showing an investor that there is a good opportunity for them to make money.

Scale

The potential for significant growth in your market is often referred to as 'scale' and this is a term that is commonplace in investment communities. If your market (and hence your business) has no scale, then the investment has less potential to be worth more in the future.

In effect, what you are doing in this section is demonstrating the flavour of the 'pie', how big that 'pie' is, and how big it might become in future. You need not concern yourself with explaining how big a piece of this pie you intend to take at this stage; this will be covered later in the plan, in the 'Financials' chapter. Your aim for now is just to convey the size of the market and its scale.

Your client base

The first step of describing your market is to define who your clients are. This will either be a specific set or group of businesses that you will sell to, or your business may sell directly to the consumer. Either way, you need to make it clear to an investor that you understand who will comprise the target market for your product or service.

In theory, this should already be clear in your mind, and it should therefore be straightforward to spell it out in your plan. If you do not have a sound fix on who your potential clients are, then you should think again before sending out any business plan or other documentation. In other words: stop and do some homework! If you are not clear about who your product or service is aimed at, your chances of success are slim to non-existent.

When I say that you should know who your clients are, I do not mean a specific list of individual company names. Rather, you should attempt to identify a specific type or set of clients.

For example, your client base may comprise companies within a specific business sector: building companies, advertising agencies, drink manufacturers, and so on. Alternatively, rather than a specific sector, your client base may be made up of businesses or types of consumer that share common characteristics. For example, your target client base might include 'All US small business with a turnover greater than $1 million and with more than 10 employees' or 'UK consumers below the age of 25'.

When we launched our asset management business in 2007 we knew precisely who our target client base was; large financial institutions that were used to investing in small funds. These included pension funds, insurance companies and endowment funds (known in financial circles as 'institutional investors'). In fact, despite what is said in the previous paragraph, we did in fact have a rather long list of names and contact numbers for particular institutions. But investors don't want to see that in a business plan – all they want to know is the general identity of your target client base.

Identify end-users

It is worth noting that if your product or service is ultimately aimed at a broad audience, but this does not in fact represent your actual direct client base, you may want to highlight this. Typically, this audience is referred to as the 'end-user'.

Let's take the book industry as an example. Books are a retail product bought by consumers. That is to say, they are bought by everyday individuals like you and me. These people are the end-users. But book publishers do not in fact sell directly to consumers. Rather, they sell in bulk to distributors, who then sell on to retail outlets such as bookshops or online stores. Sometimes a publisher may bypass a distributor and sell directly to shops. Either way, it is the shop, not the publisher, that sells the product to the consumer. So even though the consumer is the end-user, it is actually the distributors and shops that represent the publisher's client base. This type of 'chain' is certainly the norm in most retail markets. For the purpose of your plan, you should therefore be clear about who is your immediate client, differentiating them in your plan from the end-user of your product or service.

Again, let's take Pembroke Interactive as an example, given that its model is not so different from that of a book publisher.

- Pembroke Interactive heritage CD-ROMs are aimed at the retail market.
- The client base comprises principally book distributors, combined with some direct-point-of-sale vendors and shops.

Here we see that Pembroke Interactive makes retail products and therefore identifies retail consumers as the end-users. However, Pembroke Interactive does not sell their products directly to these consumers.

Some jargon terms are useful here. When your business sells directly to the consumer, it is known as B2C (business to consumer). For example, your business may be an online shop from which the public can buy products. When your business sells to other businesses, it is known as B2B (business to business).

You may have already mentioned who your client base is earlier in your business plan – if so, it will probably have been in the background section. If you haven't stated it explicitly, you may have alluded to it by mentioning distributors. Don't worry if you feel that you are repeating yourself here. It is important to emphasise on this page that you know exactly who your client base is.

Geography

When you outline your client base, make sure that you refer to any geographical regions that you intend to focus on. Typically, in the early days of your business you will focus on your domestic market. But if you are successful at home, it won't be long before you expand your horizons and want to look at similar opportunities and markets further afield. If you intend to expand abroad, you should say so here – even if that expansion lies some way in the future.

Size matters!

Once you have explained who your market consists of, you must demonstrate its size. Needless to say, investors usually like big markets, because of the potential scale! Explaining the size of your market should be relatively straightforward, but will almost certainly require some research on your part.

The commonest way of stating the size of a market is by referring to the total sales within it. Total sales means simply the sale price of a single unit multiplied by the entire number of units sold in that market. In simple terms, that means the entire value of the product or service sales for that year.

I have already mentioned my Auntie Helen, who invented a new type of mop about ten years ago. Everyone thought she was crazy to pursue her idea as a business. But, like so many entrepreneurs, she was driven by her vision and carried on despite the misgivings of others. She ignored all the doomsayers and made a success of her business. She stuck to her guns, spending tens of thousands of pounds to bring the product to life without knowing for certain that there would be a demand for it – all she had was a firm belief that it would sell.

For months she fulfilled the meagre orders that came through by making the mops herself, in an old, disused barn behind her house. One day she received an order for several thousand units from a top UK kitchenware retailer. Auntie Helen was in business and she has never looked back! It's impossible not to admire such tenacity and self-belief and I take my hat off to her.

Incidentally, the product is a stroke of genius. It is a long, thin, flexible mop that you can use to clean hard-to-reach spaces in your home, such as behind radiators and underneath fridges. It's called the 'Flatmate Duster'. There have been many imitators since then, but Flatmate is still going strong after more than twenty years.

But I digress. The point is that Auntie Helen's business plan had to include an indication of the size of the mop market, both domestically (in the UK) and internationally. To do this she needed to refer to the value of the total sales of mops in the UK and internationally. Let's say the figures were as follows:

- mop sales in UK, 2002: £35m
- mop sales globally, 2002: $543m

When you provide these numbers, always remember to give both the year that the sales relate to and the correct currency.

Market growth

The next thing you will need to show is how your market has changed over time, particularly if it has grown. Investors will want to see that you are operating in a 'growth market' – that is to say that the market your business operates in is getting bigger over time and therefore has relevant scale. Operating in a growth market will give your business a far greater chance of success, as it means that you are not swimming against the tide, so to speak.

For example, in the UK the internet is a large growth area. An online retailer is far more likely to succeed by virtue of being carried along on the 'rising tide' constituted by the ever-growing numbers of people using the internet. This contrasts sharply with other areas of the media business in the UK – most strikingly, newspaper publishing. Frankly, you would have to be barking mad to start a newspaper these days: they are simply less and less popular, with sales falling off a cliff. Anyone really determined to enter into such folly should launch as an online newspaper. You can safely assume that consumption of news on the internet, notably through smartphones, is showing dramatic growth and has huge scale.

Non-growth markets

However, just like Auntie Helen's mop, a new and innovative product that solves a genuine problem might still have a very credible chance of success in a market that is not necessarily associated with high growth. In her case, mops had been around for a long time, and the sector was not particularly a growth market. In this case, to entice the investor, Auntie Helen might have preferred to show projected growth of her own sales in contrast to those within the mop market as a whole.

The rationale here is that a new, innovative product can grow in a static or even declining market, by taking market share away from existing players and competitors.

In this case, when you are entering a static market it is worth trying to show how new products that entered the market in the past showed growth by taking existing market share. For example, the 'Vileda Supermop' made a big impact as a new type of mop back in the 1980s, stealing business away from many competitors. The point is to show that what you are offering can attract growing demand.

Market sales over time

The best way to demonstrate the growth of your market is once again to consider total sales. But this time you must look at sales over a period of several years rather than as a single snapshot of the current year. Ideally this period of time will begin in the past and then project into the future, by using expert estimates of growth in the sector.

I recommend making a short bullet point statement to this effect and then supporting this point with a chart that demonstrates such growth (assuming it is positive!). This chart will clearly reinforce your bullet point statement about the growth in your market. Remember, investors love growth!

• CD-ROM sales in UK grew 73% from 1999 to 2002

Calculating growth in percentage terms is straightforward. For example, let's say that the size of the UK internet shoe retail market was £5.6 million in 2005. By 2010 the sector had grown significantly, and was now worth £23 million. Calculate the percentage growth as shown below.

% growth of UK internet shoe retailing = (increase in value
    ÷ starting value) x 100
= ([value now – initial value] ÷ initial value) x 100
= ([23 – 5.6] ÷ 5.6) x 100 = 311%

Example

Fig. 10 reproduces a chart used in a plan, which relates to the growth of the entire US internet retail sector since 2008. It includes estimated figures for the future to 2015. This is a perfect example of a graphic representation of a growth market.

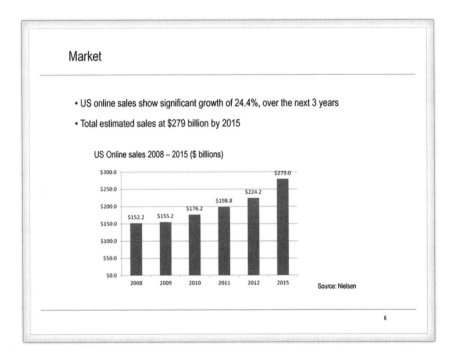

Sourcing data

But where can you find information about all of this growth in the first place? This can be the tricky part. The answer depends very much on the market that you are operating in; different markets will have different sources. But here are a few good places to start:

- **The internet** – This isn't as daft as it sounds – there is a wealth of information out there. But make sure that you use information that is available from reputable websites and do not rely on any one single source. Aim to check consistency of data from one site to the next.
- **Local libraries** – Librarians can often be invaluable for this sort of information. While librarians might not know the answer to your questions directly, they will usually know where to look for them.

- **Local business communities and organisations** – In the UK, organisations such as Business Link can point you in the right direction. Business Link is a government-funded organisation that exists specifically to help businesses set up and grow.
- **The trade press** – Most industries have regular publications that relate specifically to their area of business, known as the 'trade press' for that sector. I have called the editor of an industry's relevant leading trade magazine on several occasions to acquire market information. Because they write about the industry concerned, you can be fairly confident that they will know about its size. And if they don't, they will know someone who will. Don't be daunted by this – just pick up the phone and explain politely what you are doing. The editorial team of a trade magazine or journal is usually very helpful and interested in what is going on – that's their job! (You never know, you may even get some free publicity in the form of a story!). If you don't know what the relevant publication is, then go back a few steps to the internet, to a librarian, or to a business organisation to find out.
- **Industry specialists** – You may know someone who is already in the industry who can help – indeed, it may even be a client. They may not know the exact answers to your questions, but they will certainly be able to point you in the right direction.

If you cannot find out this information, try harder! An investor will not be impressed if you do not know or understand the market that you want to break into. Moreover, this information is fundamental to your commercial success; on discovering the detail of the actual size and growth of your market, you may realise that you are entering a sector that is not commercially worthwhile, and therefore save yourself much time, sweat and money. Alternatively, it may convince you that a fantastic opportunity lies ahead, and spur you on.

Presentation

Once you have located a source for this information and have obtained the correct numbers, make sure that you quote the source of the information and data on your plan. Typically, I will give it at the bottom of the page in a smaller font, as in **Fig. 11** overleaf.

If possible, you should always aim to present this information about your sector growth in a graphical form. Bar charts or line graphs are often ideal for this purpose. You may be able to copy an existing chart that shows industry growth from the trade press, websites or books (copyright permitting). You can then scan and paste this into your PowerPoint plan. Otherwise you will need to create your own. A simple bar chart is relatively easy to create in PowerPoint. I won't explain how to do it here; just follow the instructions that the program provides. If you are a real technophobe, find someone to do it for you: delegation is a key skill that an entrepreneur should master!

Example

Fig. 11 shows an example 'Market' page from the Wavecave plan. The title is clearly different to that which I suggest, but the message is conveyed perfectly – sales of surfing 'hard goods' are on the increase and the market is large and scalable.

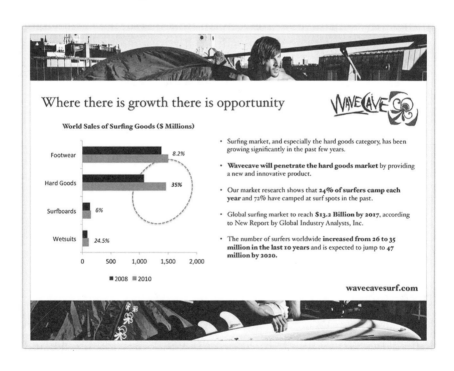

Market summary:

- Identify who your clients are.
- Specify your end-users even if they are not your clients directly. This is especially necessary for retail products and services.
- State the size of your market, in terms of sales, both domestically and internationally. Is your market big enough to be worth investing in and is it scalable?
- Demonstrate historic market growth, if you can.
- Show likely future growth, as projected by expert sources in the sector.
- Provide a graphical representation of growth.

CHAPTER 11. ROUTE TO MARKET

The previous chapter discussed your market – i.e. your potential customer base. This chapter naturally follows on from that, describing how you intend to access and sell to that customer base. The aim of the Route to Market page of your business plan is to explain the path that you will follow from production through to the point of consumption.

Not the same as 'Marketing'

Do not mistake the route to market with the much broader term 'marketing'. The concept of marketing is quite generic, covering a wide range of issues relating to how you position yourself in your sector and create awareness of your product or service in order to generate demand. Such positioning will include branding, pricing, packaging, perception and advertising. The term also covers how you communicate with and then sell to your client base.

Arguably, the route to market is just one of these marketing issues – but in the context of your business plan, it is the one that investors will want to know about first. Many books and guides on writing business plans state that a section on marketing is essential. In my view – based on experience on both sides of the fence – this is simply not the case. Investors do not want to know details about your brand or how much you will spend on advertising. It will be taken for granted that you will, in due course, develop a brand of some kind and that if the advertising spend is significant then that will emerge in the financial information later in the plan. But what an investor will want to know, in practical terms, is what path you intend to take in order to get in front of your potential clients and close a sale. This will give them a sense of your strategic approach to your market, and how scalable you believe your business opportunity to be.

Two types of route to market

There are two clear routes to market: the first is 'direct' and the second is through 'distribution', and thus 'indirect'. The latter route is also referred to in terms of 'channel partnerships' or, depending on the sector and the specifics of the business, described as 'wholesale'. Note that these two routes are not mutually exclusive, and that many businesses employ both approaches.

A direct route to market, as the name indicates, is established if a business communicates with, and sells to, the end customer directly. A few examples of businesses with a direct route to market might include law firms, restaurants or high-street shops: no other business lies between the customer paying for the service and the business providing it.

The alternative to a direct route to market is an indirect one, through the use of distribution. Rather than the product or service being sold directly to the end consumer, there are one or more intermediaries along the path from production to consumption. It might be that a distributor performs this role on a professional basis, and that this service provides their sole means of business. In many sectors this is referred to as 'wholesale distribution'. In effect, there is a professional 'middle man' in the process.

Organic Republic – the company that I mentioned earlier in the book – is specifically an organic food wholesale distributor: it buys food from farmers and producers, prepares and packages it, and then resells it to its clients across London. These clients include restaurants, sandwich shops, hotels, and so on. Organic Republic represents a clear example of a wholesale distributor in that the resale and distribution of the goods is how they make money and operate as a business.

Channel Partners

Professional wholesalers like Organic Republic are not the only option for a distribution-based route to market. Distribution may also be carried out by 'channel partners'. These are businesses that already operate in your sector, usually serving the same client base that you will be targeting, but with a different product or service. In such cases it can make sense for you to team up with a business like this, so that they offer your products or services in addition to their own. They will already be meeting and selling to your potential client base as part of their day-to-day business, and can therefore offer your product for no additional cost in the selling process. In effect, they are selling your product for you and taking a percentage of these sales. Without this you will incur costs for a salesperson, for travel, and for the direct marketing. This type of 'piggy back' distributor is often referred to as a 'channel partner'. Typically, a channel partner does not carry out wholesale distribution as its dedicated business model, but rather operates as a natural intermediary, albeit with its own product or service, within your sector.

In my mid-twenties I started a software company and I worked with a channel partner to great effect. My business was growing and I was presented with a clear choice: I could take the product to market through a concerted, direct approach, or I could find a distributor. The direct approach meant that I would have had to hire additional staff to carry out sales and marketing – and, at the time, I was concerned about whether the limited size of the market could sustain such additional costs to my business. I therefore chose to try the channel partner option and I approached several much larger players who operated in the same market, offering broadly compatible – but different – products. This arrangement made perfect sense for them, as they were already selling to precisely the market that I wished to target, and therefore would have access to many more prospects than I could ever hope to approach in the same timeframe. In return for their sales efforts, they would take a significant percentage of the sales that they generated for my software product. I had good instincts about the management of one of the businesses in particular; I felt that they were straightforward and honest. My hunch was that there would be no foul play and that they could be trusted to pay me in a timely manner, in accordance with the terms of business we had agreed. In the end, I am pleased to say that things went so well that they ended up buying my company! That's the power of a successful channel partnership. A good channel partner can eliminate a lot of upfront risk for a small business, and can often hit a market much more efficiently than you could on your own.

Distribution risks

Although this story is a great example of a channel partnership that worked, I urge you to tread carefully when entering distribution arrangements. The old adage, 'If you want something done properly, then do it yourself', often holds true. Therefore, make sure that you trust the channel partner involved and take any grand promises they might make with a pinch of salt until you see some actual results. Moreover, always ensure that you have clear break clauses in any agreement. These will allow you to get out of the deal if your channel partner fails to generate the anticipated sales. This is especially important if you enter an exclusive distribution arrangement, whereby you can only sell within a specified territory through this particular distributor or channel partner. The bottom line is that you should make sure you have a 'get out of jail free' card in case the relationship goes wrong. If you don't, it might cost you your business.

Indeed, although I had a very successful channel partnership in place when running my software company, I have certainly come out badly from relationships with other distributors and channel partners in the past. One such 'distributor' of software owed my business more than £40,000 at one point. They used the money for their own purposes and eventually went bust. I was left high and dry, and there was nothing I could do about it. In fact, the only option I had was to write off such misfortune to experience – there was no point in taking a bankrupt company to court! Subsequently, I was never quite as flexible or forgiving when it came to payment terms and conditions – and if a payment became overdue then I would get on the case immediately and work out what was going on before the problem got out of hand. It is no bad thing to learn such lessons when young. But if you get it wrong, it can cost you a lot of money – or, even worse, you might go bust.

Detail on a direct route to market

In your business plan you must make it clear which route to market you will take: direct, indirect, or both.

If you choose the direct route, it is important to provide some detail and to explain what implications this has for your business.

1. **Sales and marketing team** – The direct approach means that you will be communicating with and selling to customers with no input from any intermediaries. This means that your business will have someone (or a team, depending on the size of the business) who is

responsible for sales and marketing. You should make this clear in your business plan by outlining how many people are responsible for this role and how you expect this number to increase over time as sales increase.

2. **Who you sell to and where** – It may seem that this question goes over ground already covered in the Market chapter; but here you are focusing specifically on where your direct sales are targeted within that market.

For example, let's say that you are an Italian shoe manufacturer and that your market is the European shoe-shop sector. Rather than working through a distributor, you are selling directly to the shoe shops[*]. If you are a small business and currently have only one salesperson, it would be implausible that this salesperson would be responsible for selling directly into every shoe shop in Europe, due to the overwhelming number of shops that exist in this territory. It would make a great deal more commercial sense for this salesperson to cover a specific territory, and a specific type of shop within that territory – for example, all shoe shops in any city with more than 100,000 inhabitants, located anywhere in northern Italy and the south-east of France.

In effect, you are defining the specific focus of your sales effort and the extent of the territory within which your direct sales will take place. This will indicate to an investor the level of 'sales efficiency' that you are aiming for, and how realistic you are about your ability to sell to your market. Indeed, there is no point in stating that your business addresses an enormous market if the limited size of your sales force prevents you from reaching the whole of that market.

Detail on an indirect route to market

Your preferred route to market may be through distributors or channel partners. If so, the message that you need to convey in your

---

[*] You could argue that a shop is in itself a form of distribution to the consumer, but an industry such as shoe retail will be rife with distributors to the shops – and so, for the sake of this example, let's leave the consumer out and assume that the shop is the end-point in your business chain.

plan is broadly similar to that under the direct approach: outline the number, type and geographical location of the distributors you plan to operate with.

1. **Who your distributors are and where they operate** – State whether your distributor is a professional wholesaler or a channel partner. If you are working with channel partners, it may be relevant to explain what they offer in the sector, and why this offers you a good opportunity for distribution.

   Just as you had to outline details of your sales team under the direct route, you should make it clear who your distributors are – especially if they are big names or market leaders – and how many of them you work with. You should also mention which territories they will cover on your behalf. This will give an investor a sense of what sort of scale you are working towards and whether you can genuinely operate on an international level.

2. **Relationship with your distributor** – Investors will also want to know the nature of the relationship you have with your distributors and channel partners. There are several broad options:

   i.   Intensive – with many distributors across many territories
   ii. Selective – with fewer distributors and a closer, more focused working relationship
   iii. Exclusive – with only one distributor covering a defined territory, which precludes others from selling your product or service in this defined area

Combining both routes to market

It is possible – and in fact, common – for businesses to adopt a combination of both the direct and indirect routes to market. This often works well when a business has a wide potential market but currently has only a small, and therefore manageable number of clients, with whom it has a very close commercial relationship. These close relationships result in a consistent flow of regular sales. Combining this direct approach for the solid, regular customers with a much broader approach through distribution partners allows the business to capture more of the market than might otherwise be the case, with no danger of valuable, existing clients being neglected.

This was certainly our approach with the CD-ROM business. We would deal with and supply the heritage site shops directly. This made perfect sense, as there were relatively few of these shops. Moreover, being located at the actual heritage site itself, they naturally generated a far higher proportion of sales than a less specialised retail outlet.

For example, one product we produced was a CD-ROM about Admiral Nelson's battleship, *HMS Victory*. Since the ship served more than 500,000 visitors per year, it made perfect sense for us to target the tourist shop, located directly next to the ship. However, for wider distribution to bookshops, model-making shops, mail-order catalogues, internet retail sites and any other points of sale, we operated through distributors. The rationale was that the sales process for dealing directly with hundreds of different retail outlets would very quickly become inefficient, especially when we might only be sending batches of five to ten CD-ROMs at a time. Far better to sell a batch of one hundred to a distributor and be done with it!

Introduce the route to market

When you present information about your route to market in your plan, be sure to include an introductory line that describes whether your approach is direct, indirect, or a combination. This may seem a little obvious, but if you omit such information then the context of the rest of the information that you present on the slide may be unclear. Next, list the details that I have outlined in this chapter in the usual bullet point format. If your route to market is based on the combination approach, break the slide down into two blocks of bullet points, with an introductory line explaining the nature of the route to market for each block.

Example

Fig. 12 on the page opposite shows an example of a Route to Market page.

- Direct
    - Direct sales made specifically to UK heritage site retail outlets and several key volume retailers (e.g. Amazon)
    - All other sales are indirect through distributors
    - David Bateman, Director, responsible for direct sales

- Indirect
    - 3 main distribution territories: UK, N. America, Australasia
    - Distributors include Gardners Books in UK; N. America has 5 distributors operating
    - Non-exclusive, selective distribution approach – only work with wholesale distributors that order minimum annual volumes, in batches of 100 CD-ROMs

7

Route to Market summary:

- Do not confuse 'route to market' with 'marketing'. Investors do not want to know about your advertising campaigns, branding, and so on. What they want to know is how you will access and sell to your clients. Keep to this point.
- Define your route to market: is it direct, indirect or a combination?
- If your approach is direct, then show your sales resources and the specific segment of the market you are targeting. Remember to show geographical information as well.
- If your approach is indirect, be clear about whether the intermediaries are wholesale distributors or channel partners.
- State who your main distributors are, the number of distributors, and their relevant territories.
- State the nature of your relationship with your distributors and channel partners: is it intensive, selective, or exclusive?
- A combination of both routes is perfectly acceptable and indeed common. Break your page up into two relevant blocks and address each route to market accordingly.

CHAPTER 12. COMPETITION

The objective of this page in your business plan is, as its title suggests, to give a clear outline of your competition. A further aim is to demonstrate what position you plan to achieve in the context of this competition.

Do not avoid the subject

Drawing attention to your competition may seem a little counterintuitive – you might think that you don't want to show an investor the number and variety of businesses operating in the same space as you, as it may put them off making an investment. But if an investor is seriously interested in your business, they will inevitably do some homework of their own and quickly unearth any competition that is out there. If you omit such information from your plan, investors will only ask you about it anyway. If so, it may seem that either you are deliberately withholding it from them or that you don't properly understand your business sector. Either way, there is really no benefit in failing to provide information about your competition.

Define competition

What exactly is a competitor? The answer seems obvious: a competitor is another business that offers a product or service that is similar to your own. In some cases the competition may offer exactly the same product or service. In other cases, such as Auntie Helen's mop, no one else sold a product that was similar but standard mops were already big business. This clearly represented competition in the sense that she would be trying take sales from the businesses already producing standard mops.

At this stage, there is no need to focus on subtle differences between you and your competition: you should simply consider all businesses that operate in a similar area, with similar products or services, as your competition.

It is not helpful to offer a long, boring list of all your competitors. You must, of course, be aware of them all and understand what they do; this is necessary for your business to succeed. But an investor will not need that level of detail at this stage. The best way to present information about your competition is in fact to summarise the broader landscape in two or three concise statements and then provide a little more detail on the main players.

If you get this right, you can draw attention to the opportunity that the competition represents for your business. For example, if a business sector has lots of small competitors, it may be easier to break into. The presence of competition in a market shows that there is an established demand for your product or service, which is clearly a good thing. Just because there is competition it does not mean that there is not room for more players. If there is no competition it might even put some investors off, as it could imply that your business is not viable and that you have misread the commercial opportunity.

Introduce the competition

The competition page in your plan should start with general statements that describe the overall state of the competition, and then highlight any leaders in the sector. Taking the example of the CD-ROM business, the statements would look something like this:

- Many small, privately owned multimedia companies offer generalist CD-ROM production services.
- Two key leaders: Dorling Kindersley for general knowledge subjects; Montparnasse Multimedia, specialising in the heritage sector in France.

You should then provide more detailed information – especially if it demonstrates that the market you are operating in offers clear opportunities for business. In competition with our CD-ROM business, Montparnasse Multimedia had shown the good sense to create a CD-ROM of the Louvre museum in Paris. It was an immediate success, selling more than 1 million copies in total – an incredible result. It occurred to us that, if they could do it in France, we would have a perfectly good chance of achieving similar success with a major British heritage site (the British Museum? Buckingham Palace? Stonehenge?).

Competition points to potential

If your competitors have been very successful in a field with unexploited potential remaining, it is essential to underline that fact:

* Montparnasse Multimedia sold >1 million copies of the 'Le Louvre' CD-ROM, representing retail sales >£13 million.

This demonstrates a clear potential for success to your investor. If you spot an opportunity to create this kind of association in the mind of your investor, do not hesitate to take it.

No competition

But what if you feel that you have no competition? This is highly unlikely. If your product or service is truly innovative or you are genuinely the first to be doing something, then this section may seem a little redundant. However, it is often the case that a new product or service is an improvement on something that already exists, and that your competition is thus represented by the older, less effective version. For example, British inventor James Dyson did not invent the vacuum cleaner, but he did invent a new way for it to operate. Manufacturers of the older type of vacuum cleaner represented his competition because he would need to take business away from them. As we saw, the same was true for Auntie Helen's new type of mop.

Visuals and graphics

If possible, it is worth demonstrating the competitive landscape visually, with a graph or chart. It should show the percentage of the market held by each of the major competitors. Smaller, fragmented competitors can be brought together under the heading of 'others'. A pie chart often works well for this purpose.

I have seen several business plans that show the competition, and where their own business sits in the context of this competition, in a matrix format. This format works especially well if you are demonstrating the different strengths and weaknesses of the competition, or perhaps what part of the sector they operate in. A matrix allows you to categorise them accordingly, in a visual format.

Example

Fig. 13 demonstrates an example of a competition matrix for a communications software company. This company provides software to businesses that enables employees to access 'group messaging'. This means that many users can follow the thread of a conversation that would otherwise be in an email. This is advantageous because people do not inadvertently miss the information or can choose to ignore if it is not relevant to them. It also means that everyone in a team has access to the same information, which is particularly useful for call centres or sales centres. The matrix below shows the competitive landscape and where the company fits in. You can clearly see that the system is aimed specifically at the business 'Enterprise' sector. This is contrasted in the matrix with products in a broader retail market, such as Skype.

Competition summary:

- Do your homework. Investors want to know about your competition, so include this information in the plan.
- Don't just list competitors. Begin by summarising the competitive landscape.
- If your market has a few dominant players, focus principally on them. Outline their similarities with your own business, as well as their geographical location and give their sales figures.
- Show where you are positioned relative to this competition. Do you do exactly the same as them or do you operate in a different way, or in a slightly different space?
- Present the competition graphically if you can. A pie chart or a matrix works well.
- Turn a potentially awkward subject into a positive point. Use the competition to demonstrate your business's potential.

CHAPTER 13. MANAGEMENT

If you ask anyone looking to invest in a business for the most important criteria, I can guarantee that one of them will be its 'people'. By the term 'people', or 'management', I mean the individuals who run the business; the people who have taken the risk of starting the business and who make the decisions about where the business is going.

In this context, 'management' does not refer to middle managers who have been hired to carry out specific roles in the business. Rather, it means those who are typically the owners of the business or those who sit on the board of directors – usually people in senior positions, such as the CEO (chief executive officer), COO (chief operating officer), sales and marketing director, CTO (chief technology officer), and so on.

The titles that people adopt within businesses can sometimes be quite amusing – especially in larger organisations, where titles seem to bestow some mystical status on their holders. In an investment bank there are hundreds of so-called 'managing directors', many of whom manage no more than five or six people! Here it is also easy to find several 'global heads' of various different functions within a single business unit.

I recall a miserable year spent in the prison-like confines of an investment bank. The system of titles had become so ridiculous and self-aggrandising that a colleague, with his tongue firmly in his cheek, had business cards printed identifying him as 'global head of global'. Needless to say, although his clients found it entertaining, his superiors were less amused. His initiative was promptly quashed, and he was duly issued with more sensible cards. The essential point is that, while titles can be helpful, you shouldn't risk seeming pretentious. If there are only two of you in the business, then the term CEO for one of you may seem a little far-fetched.

Good management is crucial

It is clear that investors value good management. Indeed, the people running a business will inevitably make or break it, no matter how good or bad the product or service might be. You might have the best product available, but if the team that runs the business is not up to scratch, it simply won't succeed. The execution of a business is without doubt more important than the nature of the product or the service itself. A potential investor will therefore take a very close look at the management of a business.

Prior experience

So what does an investor look for in a good manager or management team? First, they look for relevant experience and an understanding of the type of business concerned. For example, if you are starting a software company they will want to see that you have experience in technology, and ideally knowledge of the specific business sector that you are operating in. Relevant experience is possibly one of the most important aspects of the skill set that a management team has to offer.

Such experience must be demonstrated on this page of your business plan. Include the names of relevant companies that your management team has worked for previously, and the roles that were performed. Blue-chip companies and well-established names are particularly helpful here. Note the word 'relevant': investors do not want to hear about the cheese shop that you worked in as a Saturday sales assistant when you were fifteen years old!

If you do not have direct sector experience in a formal work environment, don't worry. That is often the case with young entrepreneurs. The founders of Facebook or Microsoft hadn't even finished studying at university when they launched their businesses. If you have no relevant formal employment experience, just be sure to emphasise that you have experienced the sector in other ways. For example, you could demonstrate that you have been a regular user of products currently available in the sector, and therefore understand the opportunity through first-hand experience. As an example, the Wavecave business plan clearly shows that the management team are all avid surfers.

Alongside direct sector experience, broader commercial experience is also valuable – for example, having started a business in the past, and in particular having made a return for investors. Likewise, having occupied a senior position of responsibility in a well-established firm can count for a lot, particularly where that position included being in charge of a team.

Teamwork

Investors will always approve if the plan includes a management team that has worked together in the past. This means that they are more likely to know each other's strengths and weaknesses, and that there is less chance of harmful internal disputes and conflicts. Partnerships are complicated and difficult to manage, especially when money is involved. Internal disharmony is often a cause of business inefficiency and sometimes outright failure. A management team is subject to the same pressures and stresses as any other sort of team.

Not all businesses will have a management team in place, especially those in the early stages. At first it might just be you, or perhaps two of you as partners (although that is arguably already a team!). If this is the case, it is a perfectly acceptable situation and it will not necessarily deter investors who are used to investing in nascent and early-stage businesses. But be aware that, should your business grow, you will at some point need to hire people to share the workload and a management team will inevitably be established. Even if that team is not made up of direct owners of the business, its members will invariably have certain decision-making responsibilities that can affect the business as a whole. They should therefore be considered part of the team in the context of a business plan.

Education

After your experience, education may also be of interest to investors. I have what is possibly a controversial view on this: I believe that most education is largely irrelevant to doing business. You only achieve a proper understanding of business through actually doing business; the type of instruction that you usually find in textbooks and lectures is largely irrelevant (I acknowledge the irony here, given that I am writing a book on business!). Business is a skill, and you can only learn a skill by doing it. For example, I could learn the theory behind playing a saxophone from a book; but I can only learn how to play the saxophone by practising. Business is no different.

Therefore, in your business plan education should be treated as secondary to experience. Although academic achievement indicates that you are bright, it tells an investor nothing at all about how good you will be at running a business. Intelligence comes in many forms and academic prowess is just one of them. In business, I would give far greater weight to emotional intelligence and the ability to communicate effectively.

Don't misunderstand me. Education is fundamental to a healthy society, and further education for the simple joy of learning is a wonderful thing. Moreover, it can engender intellectual confidence and encourage curiosity – both invaluable characteristics. But it won't teach you how to build a business. Look at Richard Branson. He has no qualifications to speak of. Neither does Auntie Helen. The majority partner in our $4 billion investment fund has, as far as I know, no qualifications at all – certainly not a degree. So don't worry if you feel under-qualified. It is experience that counts, followed by a straightforward drive to succeed.

Having said all that, not all investors share my view. Some place a high value on relevant qualifications. With this in mind, if you have some formal qualification that is relevant to your business then you should make that clear.

Strictly relevant

As you must give an overview of all of the principal members of the management team, you will have limited space available. Consequently, I would suggest observing a fairly strict notion of 'relevance' when it comes to education and qualifications. For example, if you are launching a software company, I would consider computer sciences or mathematics to be relevant – but certainly not Classics or theology. Likewise, feel free to include top-name universities if you wish. Elitist as it might seem, some investors are impressed by such things.

Awards and accolades

If you have received any awards or accolades in relation to your business expertise, they are well worth including here if you have the space. Auntie Helen, for example, was nominated Business Woman of the Year in the 1990s – not bad going for someone who had started from scratch with no educational qualifications to speak of.

Non-executive directors

The inclusion of non-executive directors is a great way of bringing industry experience to your management team. 'Non-execs' should be experienced professionals, having worked for many years in a sector that is relevant to your business. If you have them, make sure that you include them on this slide.

Non-execs often work in an advisory capacity, rather than as day-to-day participants in the business. They offer strategic guidance, contacts and expertise. They also provide a layer of comfort for investors, because the non-execs often have a responsibility for corporate governance and are there to put a stop to any corporate misconduct that might take place behind the scenes.

If you have a well-known member of the business community on your board as a non-exec, it provides a valuable endorsement for your business. An industry veteran is unlikely to want to associate their name and reputation with a management team that they feel is unlikely to succeed.

Presentation

Putting all of this information into a format that works in your plan is straightforward, and broadly follows the bullet point format of all the previous pages.

However, I recommend one subtle departure from the format of preceding slides. With each member of the management team that you present on the slide, you should include the person's name and title as a non-bullet pointed line, so that it acts as a clear subtitle. You should follow this name with preferably no more than three bullet points – four at most – outlining experience, awards and education.

You may feel that three bullet points provides nowhere near enough space to impress upon an investor what an amazing individual you are. But you must remember that your plan is a quick 'elevator' pitch, in which your objective is to convey your message as quickly and efficiently as possible. Much as we all like to talk about ourselves, you must keep this content brief. If an investor is genuinely interested in your business then they will inevitably ask for more information about your background, or perhaps a comprehensive CV, later in the investment process. Remember, your business plan is the bait to get an investor hooked in the first place. You can reel them in with the detail later.

Another reason to keep it snappy is that if you are working as a management team with others, you will need to include their details as well. If you are not careful, the page can get very busy, which usually makes an investor unlikely to read it. I recommend an absolute maximum of four people per slide. If your management team comprises more than four then I suggest you create a second slide to follow on from the management slide – 'Management (continued)' – and then pick up from where you left off on the previous page, using the same format for each member of the team.

Some people like to add photos of each person next to the bullet point 'mini biographies' – preferably just appropriate head shots. I have no strong view on this. If you are particularly attractive, maybe you feel it could make a difference. But as I'm never going to sell a business on my looks, I prefer to restrict myself to text for these purposes.

Since you are trying to include a considerable amount of information on this page – possibly more than any other – it is worth adjusting the formatting accordingly. For the bullet point text, I recommend slightly reducing the point-size and line-spacing of your text. Take a look at how the content looks on your page, and make a sensible judgment yourself. As ever, if you are unsure that you've achieved a suitable look, refer to the free, editable template at www.businessplansthatgetinvestment.com, and experiment with it.

Don't give your life story

I have one further tip here that relates to a common trend I have noticed in the business deals I have been involved in over the years. When you meet someone that you may be making a deal with, particularly if you are the investor, there will inevitably come a point when introductions are made and your counterpart across the table is asked to offer up his or her background. This moment acts as an invaluable litmus test of whether or not this is the sort of person you should do business with. If they spend the next fifteen minutes droning on about all of their amazing achievements, I have noticed that business is rarely done and if it is, it is usually bad business. That might sound arbitrary, but for me it has become a reliable barometer of how likely I am to be able to work with someone. Those people with a real talent for business often feel very little need to talk about themselves. So, if an investor asks you about your background, keep it succinct and relevant – just like the plan. If they want more, they will dig deeper or ask for a CV.

Example

Finally, let's take a look at an example. **Fig. 14** represents the 'Management' page from a business plan for a new software company (the company is real, but sadly the beautiful people are not!). Even with just four members of the team listed on this page, with only three key points each, you can see how busy the page can get. When you write your own plan, if you feel that this page is becoming too crowded, do not hesitate to create an additional page to make space for the team details.

Management summary:

- Investors like to see direct, relevant experience in a management team. Demonstrate this experience if you have it. You must show that you understand your business space.
- Demonstrate broader business experience if possible. Examples include previous business ownership, positions of responsibility, managing teams, etc.
- Include relevant education.
- Include awards and accolades.
- Ensure that you highlight experienced non-executive board members, should you have them.
- Do not overcrowd the page. If necessary, adjust the formatting and use a continuation page.
- Keep it brief. If an investor wants to know more, they will ask.

CHAPTER 14. BUSINESS MODEL

This next part of your business plan explains your 'business model'. This term refers to the various steps in the process of your product or service being created and sold. This means that you need to show each step from initial production all the way through to final sale, and sometimes beyond. It is important that you include this in your plan, because you will not only outline the steps in the process, but also identify the costs or revenues associated with each step. This will enable an investor to understand the basic structure through which your business makes money, which is fundamental to their ability to make an investment decision.

Steps

There is a sequence of steps when you create and sell a product or service. It's useful here to return to the example of my CD-ROM business. Since it is now an outdated business in an area that no longer exists due to advances in technology, the financial figures are no longer commercially sensitive. Note that information in your business model is naturally quite sensitive, because if your suppliers or customers can see your costs and revenues it may give them some negotiating power and give them an advantage over you at the next meeting.

The CD-ROM business model consisted of the following steps:

1. CD-ROM print and packaging: cost 80p per unit
2. Delivery to distributor/retailer: cost 10p per unit
3. Sale to distributor/retailer: revenue average approximately £5 per unit
4. Final retail price: £14.99 per unit

As you can see, this straightforward list explains in concise, simple terms how much each CD-ROM costs to make and deliver, and then how much each one is sold for. It also shows the final retail price. This is your business model: each step leads to the next.

Follow the stages to the end-user

Note that it is important to include the final sale price of your product or service, especially if it is a retail product. By final sale price, I mean the price that the end-user pays for it. For example, if the product that you manufacture is for retail then you will probably sell it to a distributor. But that is not where the chain stops, as the distributor then sells the product to a retailer, who in turn sells to a customer. It is the final price charged to the customer that you should show.

This information gives an investor a sense of how you are positioning yourself in the market, and whether your product or service is more expensive or cheaper than those of your direct competitors. For example, £14.99 was, and still is, quite a lot of money for a book. However, it was a fairly standard price at the time for a CD-ROM. This would give an investor a sense of where the CD-ROM is positioned in the market, relative to paperback book sales.

Consistent principles

You should apply the same principles outlined here for the CD-ROM business model to your own business plan. Some businesses may have straightforward business models. For example, a product-based business model is easy: you explain it in terms of units of the product. How much does it cost you to make each unit? How much do you sell each unit for?

Conversely, for some businesses the business model may not be so easy to articulate. For example, a management consultancy sells its expertise. This is straightforward enough. However, if this service is delivered by employees of the business, they represent an associated cost – just as the manufacture of a CD-ROM does in the above example. A management consultant might charge their clients a daily rate – so, for the business model to be as clear as possible, you could show your employment costs on the same daily basis.

There are various ways of quantifying the costs and revenues in your business model, but broadly speaking you should compare like with like. If you think of your revenue as being generated by sales of units, then you should aim to think of your costs on a per-unit basis as well. This is important in order to make your business model clear for the reader.

If this seems a little confusing, a useful tip here is to present your business model using the same terms that you outline in your invoices to clients. For example, we would charge distributors for CD-ROMs on a per-unit basis, usually in batches of 100; the business model was therefore presented in units. Consultancies, on the other hand, typically charge day rates; it therefore makes sense to present the model in terms of daily costs and revenues. At our investment fund we would charge fees as a percentage of the assets that we managed – so that would provide the framework for putting together the business model.

Mark-up

This page on your plan does not need much more information than what I have already outlined. Sometimes I like to insert a couple of introductory bullet points before itemising the steps in the model. These bullet points have two purposes: the first is to explain the 'mark-up', and the second is to mention briefly how the model will change with an increase in sales volume.

The term 'mark-up' is very common in business, and relates to the difference between the amount that it costs you to make or provide a product or service, and the amount for which you sell it. A mark-up can be given as a nominal amount. In the case of the CD-ROMs, it cost a total of 90p to make and deliver one unit. The average sale price to our distributor was £5.00. The mark-up was therefore £4.10 (£5.00 – £0.90).

But mark-up figures are often expressed in percentage terms. Calculating this number is straightforward:

mark-up percentage = (increase in price ÷ cost price) x 100
= ([sale price – cost price] ÷ cost price) x 100
= ([£5 – £0.9] ÷ £0.9) x 100 = 456%

So, for every unit we produced we were making a mark-up of 456%! That's not bad – and it's why I liked the business so much. I think that sort of mark-up, if scalable, would make any investor sit up and pay attention. Note here that the mark-up percentage is not the same as the profit percentage. We'll talk about profit later – but do not get the two confused. They are not the same.

Changes in mark-up and economy of scale

The second introductory bullet point here will typically refer to how much your mark-up changes when there is a significant increase in the number of sales of your product or service. If you are producing greater numbers of your product or providing greater amounts of your service, then the costs per unit of providing these goods or services should come down. This is usually encapsulated in the phrase 'economy of scale'.

Printing and selling books provides a good demonstration of an economy of scale. If you compare the cost of printing 1,000 books to that of printing 2,000, you will find that the cost for 2,000 is less than double that for 1,000. This is because the initial cost of setting up the printing machine is the same for one book, 100 books or 2,000 books. It must be done irrespective of the number of books that there are to be printed. However, once this initial cost is covered the only additional cost is for the paper, ink and energy consumed. The incremental amount per unit therefore decreases the more you print, because the initial cost is spread out over the number of units printed, and the mark-up increases accordingly.

Let me demonstrate this with some numbers:

Books printed (units)	1,000	2,000	5,000
Printer set-up (£)	1,000	1,000	1,000
Paper (£ per unit)	1	0.90	0.80
Ink (£ per unit)	0.60	0.55	0.50
Energy (£ per unit)	0.40	0.38	0.35
Total cost of print	£3,000	£4,660	£9,250
Sale price (£ per unit)	4	4	4
Total sale price (£)	£4,000	£8,000	£21,000
Mark-up	33%	72%	127%

You can see from the example that as more units are printed, the cost per unit of the materials such as paper and ink also reduces. This is because the materials can be bought in bulk, which means that there is a price discount. Such volume purchasing, and the corresponding price reductions, contributes further to the economy of scale (and the resultant mark-up).

As you can see from the table, an economy of scale means that your mark-up increases, which is good news. If your model has this sort of profile, you should be sure to emphasise that in an introductory bullet point, so that an investor will immediately understand how the business becomes more attractive as volumes increase. You should clearly state how much your mark-up increases with each increment in volume.

Recurring revenue

A final point that requires emphasis, if it is relevant to your business model, is the concept of 'recurring revenue'. Investors will always be drawn to businesses that exhibit recurring revenue, and including this detail in your business model will inevitably increase the chances of investment success.

'Recurring revenue' refers to the process whereby the initial sale of a product or service then goes on to generate further sales in the future. B2B software businesses are a good example of this. In the model that is usually adopted, a sale is made only once to the client but, rather than a one-off fee, the client is charged on an annual basis, year after year. It is almost like an ongoing lease. A B2C example of a business with recurring revenue might be a dentist's clinic. Unless the client moves away from the local area or switches to a different clinic, they will keep coming back indefinitely.

From an investor's perspective, this recurring-revenue model is very attractive: it demonstrates the future security of the business by providing a stable cash flow.

Presentation

At this stage, do not try to explain your business model in terms of the time taken from one step to the next, nor its profitability. Those issues are covered on the next page of your plan. Just keep to explaining the sale price of your product or service and the cost of producing and providing it to your clients.

You can present your business model in two ways. The first is much like the standard bullet point structure, but with steps that follow the introductory bullet points. The second is presentation in a table. This format works well if you want to emphasise significant changes in mark-up with different increments in sales volume, much like the example of book printing.

Example

For an example of the steps process, see **Fig. 15** below. Alternatively, you can present this same information in a table format.

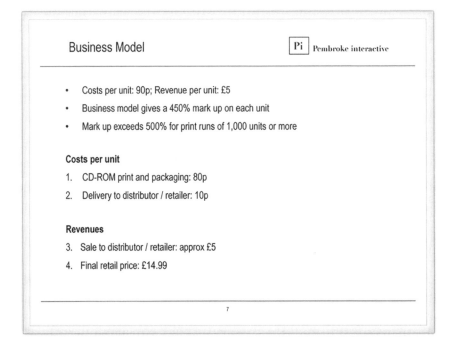

Business model summary:

- Show an investor, in clear and simple terms, how your business makes money.
- Clearly demonstrate the steps in the 'life' of your product or service, from production/provision through to sale, including end-user prices. Make sure that you keep these steps simple

and easy to follow. Each step must logically lead to the next one.

- Articulate these steps in financial terms also – as costs or revenues.
- Demonstrate your 'mark-up' in percentage terms.
- If relevant, show how mark-up will grow as sales volumes increase.
- If your model incorporates recurring revenue, it is very important to emphasise this fact. This point is absolutely crucial because any recurring revenue can have a huge impact on the value that an investor places on your business and whether it is even appealing to them in the first place.
- Focus on the business model because simplicity is key. Ignore issues such as the amount of time it might take to implement the model, and do not confuse this model with profit – they are not the same.

CHAPTER 15. FINANCIALS

Providing a written explanation of the financial workings of a business is something that makes many people apprehensive. You might well feel that you don't have the relevant expertise. But you don't need to know about accounting or have a business qualification to be able to produce the financial figures required for a business plan.

Contrary to popular opinion, a business plan does not need to include extensive, detailed financial projections and assumptions. Investors prefer to see a few clear, well-considered key figures in the plan, rather than page after page of numbers. If they are interested then they may ask for some more detailed numbers later on, but let's not forget the point of the plan in the first place: to grab the investor's attention, so that they want to get involved.

Demonstrate growth

So what do you need to show an investor on this page of the plan? First of all, you need to demonstrate that your business is going to grow in the next few years. This growth will make your investors the return on their money. If there is no clear potential for growth in your business, it is almost impossible to secure an investment.

The best way to show this growth is to display the information in a table, with columns representing each year. I suggest providing projected figures a minimum of three and a maximum of five years into the future.

The rows of the table should display only key financial data. An investor will not want to see detailed financial planning at this stage – they will have no interest in how much you intend to spend on coffee for the office every year, nor what your photocopying costs might be. What they will want to see are the crucial reference points that will give them a feel as to whether or not your business can be scaled up, whether it fits the kind of financial profile they are looking for, and whether your future projections are realistic, and not just pie-in-the-sky fantasies.

Giving this 'feel' is important. Just because you write down what you expect your future sales and other figures to be doesn't mean an investor will agree with you. If they are seriously interested in your proposal they will want to research some facts and figures for themselves and thus will invariably take most of what you say with a pinch of salt. Are you a dreamer who makes up numbers to fit your dreams, or are you someone who has really done their homework and gained a sense of what is really going on in your sector?

You should insert years in the top row of your table, and identify key financial metrics down the left-hand column. Amazingly, there are only three metrics that are essential (see Table 1).

Table 1

Year	2012	2013	2014	2015
Revenue				
Gross Profit				
Net Profit				

It's as simple as that! To give an investor what they need at this early stage, you need only three types of data:

1. Revenue
2. Gross profit
3. Net profit

This will give the reader a very quick snapshot of the information they need. Remember, by explaining your business model earlier in your plan, you have already given some important information at a more detailed level. Now you are providing a broader financial overview of the business as a whole, both now and into the future.

Financial metrics: Revenue

I will now explain each of these key financial metrics in turn. The first figure is 'Revenue'. This refers to the total amount of sales that you make in a given year. For example, let's say that your business is a product manufacturer. This is how you calculate the revenue figure:

number of products sold x price per product = revenue

So, for the CD-ROM business, Pembroke Interactive sold the product to the distributor for £5 per unit, and we felt that it was fair to assume that we would sell around 10,000 units in the second year of trading, once the first two CD-ROMs had been produced. Therefore, our revenue estimate for the second year was:

10,000 x £5 = £50,000

The revenue for a restaurant will be the total sales of food and drink in a year; for a law firm, it will be the total number of billable hours for the year; and so on.

It is important to say that the future figures are estimates, so that it is almost impossible to be exact. Therefore I always prefer to use round numbers when making estimates and projections. Giving a precise number – such as 97,326 units sold next year instead of 100,000 – is pointless. Remember that investors are looking at these numbers not only to get a sense of the potential scale of your business, but also as a way to get a feel for whether you are making sensible estimates.

Investors will not believe your figures until they have done their own homework. Giving rounded numbers demonstrates that you understand that these are estimates, and that you are not making naively precise predictions; it shows that you are sensible and pragmatic. Nevertheless, you should not be too conservative with your estimates, as that will also be detrimental to your cause. You should think big, but always remain realistic.

So how can you be realistic if the numbers you have to produce are estimates? One way of doing this is to understand the sort of numbers that your competitors produce. You can usually get a rough idea of their revenues by asking people who already work in the relevant sector.

Alternatively, you may be able to access a competitor's accounts from a government source, such as Companies House (if you're in the UK). Also, remember that you have already quantified the size of the market, in terms of revenues, earlier in your business plan. Judging your market share realistically in percentage terms should give you a guide to what your figures should be.

When you have arrived at your estimates I strongly recommend that you check them with someone who has some experience in finance, ideally in the context of your sector. This might be an accountant or a financial analyst. Listen to what they say, but remember that what they say is not gospel. Alternatively, you could talk to someone who works directly in the sector, such as a manager or a salesperson. They should be able to assess whether your numbers are realistic.

Producing these financial figures is useful not only for investors, but also you. They can serve as an excellent reality check, and make you carefully think through what you are doing. It is easy to get carried away by what seems like a great idea. Follow your heart and use your instincts, by all means, but also let your head have a say in these matters. If the numbers do not stack up to produce a viable business then you must be honest with yourself and address the issue.

Financial metrics: Gross profit

In Table 1 (shown previously), you can see that the second relevant figure is 'gross profit'. This is calculated as:

revenue − cost of sales = gross profit

In order to reach the gross profit figure, you must understand and calculate the 'cost of sales'. Despite the mysterious name, 'cost of sales' is in fact simple to establish. If you have written the 'Business Model' page of your business plan, the good news is that you already know this figure! Put simply, 'cost of sales' refers to the direct costs involved in making your product or offering your service, excluding all other peripheral costs. To be clear, it relates to just those costs that are directly involved in production and/or provision. Direct costs contrast with indirect costs, which are more to do with the general running costs of the business. Indirect costs are often referred to as 'overheads'.

Let's illustrate this by looking at the cost of sales of three different types of business:

1. A CD-ROM producer's direct costs include the costs of printing and packaging each CD-ROM.
2. A restaurant's direct costs include the cost of ingredients and drinks.
3. A Wavecave manufacturer's direct costs include the cost of fabrics and materials, and the payment of an external manufacturing business to produce each unit.

These businesses have different direct costs, but they will inevitably have many indirect costs in common. These will include salaries, office expenses, marketing, travel, and so on. Such indirect costs are not part of the business model that you outlined earlier on in the plan. If you are not sure whether a cost constitutes part of your cost of sales, it may help to refer back to your business model: if the cost is part of your business model, then it is almost certainly part of your cost of sales.

By applying this approach to the table on this page of your plan you can see that the slightly amended calculation below gives you your gross profit figure. Simply subtract the total of all of your direct costs from the revenue number for the same year:

revenue − direct costs = gross profit

I confess that the word 'simply' may turn out to be a little misleading in practice. Establishing all of your direct costs for a particular year may in fact be more difficult than it sounds, but the easiest method is to use a spreadsheet.

Spreadsheets

If you do not know how to use spreadsheets, then I strongly recommend that you learn. They have many advanced functions, but for the purposes of your business plan they are very straightforward. They allow you to play with your estimates and create future scenarios without having to re-enter your figures each time. A spreadsheet will therefore save you a lot of time.

The results from such scenario analysis have provided a wake-up call to me on many occasions, when it has become immediately apparent that I am either being wildly optimistic or painfully conservative in my projections. Just as an athletics coach will tell their athletes that 'the stopwatch never lies', and consequently force them to be honest about their performance, calculating your costs on a spreadsheet will leave you no escape from the truth: the result is there in black and white. You may not like the number you have in front of you, but there it is.

To make your life easier, I have already created a spreadsheet to help you prepare your figures. You can download it from www.businessplansthatgetinvestment.com, and it is free for readers of this book. Why pay an accountant when I have already done this preparatory work for you?! The spreadsheet incorporates most of the fields that you will need in order to input your cost and revenue assumptions and it does all the subsequent calculations for you. You may want to add more fields or take some out, depending on your business, but this free template will give you an idea of what is needed and will get you off to a good start.

Scenario analysis

Once you have entered your figures into the spreadsheet you can change them according to different scenarios, and the spreadsheet calculations will show you what happens in each circumstance. As always, you should ask yourself if the resulting numbers are sensible – if your gross profit is shown as 95 per cent of revenue in the calculation, for example, there is probably something wrong with your assumptions!

If your revenue or profits are bigger than the percentage of the market that you can realistically take, then once again, there is clearly something wrong with your assumptions. If they are bigger than the entire market, there is definitely something wrong! Always check your numbers and make sure that they look intuitively reasonable. This is as much an art as it is a science.

As I have mentioned, an ideal way to carry out this 'sanity check' is to compare your results with those of other businesses that operate in the same sector. If your numbers are very different in percentage terms, then you should stop and ask yourself why. If you do not, I guarantee that a potential investor will.

Financial metrics: Net Profit

The final figure in your table is 'net profit'. To get to the net profit figure, you must first calculate something called 'EBITDA'. This catchy name stands for 'earnings before interest, tax, depreciation and amortisation'. What this cumbersome phrase really means is something close to the net profit number that you need, but not quite. EBITDA is the amount before you deduct interest payments on any debt and take away any tax owed (the 'interest' and 'tax' parts), and before the accountants perform their black magic on your figures and turn them into something entirely 'different' by adjusting for the 'depreciation' and 'amortisation' parts!

In order to estimate EBITDA for the purpose of your business plan, you do not need to know exactly what the details of these terms mean and the following calculation will usually suffice:

gross profit − overheads = EBITDA

You can use the free spreadsheet to list your overheads and have your EBITDA calculated for you. Remember that overheads are the equivalent of 'indirect costs' – that is to say, the costs that are not related to the direct provision of your product or service, but rather are the general costs that are associated with running the business.

The following are some examples of overheads:

- salaries
- marketing
- travel
- office space
- electricity

Derive Net Profit from EBITDA

Once you have EBITDA you must then work to make this number your net profit. Firstly, if you have an accountant helping you, you can also allow for the amortisation and depreciation. However, don't get too stuck on this as it is often irrelevant for most early-stage businesses. Secondly, you must deduct any interest payments and tax owed. The tax in this case is the corporation tax that any business must pay the government, and it is much like personal income tax that we all pay. In the UK, this tax rate is currently 20% of what your business makes.

To summarise, assuming that we don't pay too much attention to depreciation and amortisation, the net profit is calculated as follows:

EBITDA − interest on debt − corporation tax = net profit

Once you have made these changes to EBITDA, you have your net profit number ready to present in the table of your plan.

Why is net profit important to an investor?

The net profit figure that you provide in your estimates is extremely relevant to your investor for two reasons: first of all, it gives them a number on which they can compare and value the business – we'll cover the concept of valuation in the next chapter. Secondly, it shows them what they will receive each year as a dividend payment. For example, if your net profit is £10,000 and your investor owns 30% of your business, then they shall receive a dividend payment of £3,000 that year. Therefore, net profit is important because it demonstrates the potential value of the business and also how an investor might get a return on their money.

Financial Metrics: Margin

It is worth mentioning the term 'margin'. This is commonly used in business and it is crucial that you understand what it means. Indeed, it is such a common notion that I actually like to add it as another row in the table of financial metrics.

Margin is a straightforward concept. It refers to your gross and net profit figures, relative to your revenue. Margin is typically given in percentage terms, rather than in monetary terms. Presenting the information in this way enables an investor to ascertain quickly how profitable your business is relative to other businesses or sectors.

For example, a business with a 50 per cent margin would generally be deemed highly profitable, and would be inherently attractive to an investor – whereas a business with a 5 per cent margin might be less so. Of course, an investor can easily work out the margin for themselves using the absolute numbers that you provide in your table; but that would defeat the point of the plan, which is to pitch your business to them as clearly and concisely as possible. Calculating margin in percentage terms is not difficult:

gross margin = (gross profit / revenue) x 100
net margin = (net profit / revenue) x 100

Make sure that you know these numbers. It is inevitable that the subject will come up when you are presenting and talking to investors. Note that the free spreadsheet I have prepared for you will also calculate your margin numbers.

Historic growth

You are using this page in your plan to demonstrate the growth and scale of your business. So, if your business has been around for a few years and has grown over that period, you should include this information. The most efficient way to do this is to add some extra columns to your table, to the left of the current year, showing figures for previous years. Add the real, historic revenues, gross profit and net profit to the relevant cells in the table. Showing historic information is especially important if you can demonstrate historic growth. This information emphasises the 'proof of concept' that I discussed earlier in the book, and shows an investor that your business has a clear market and potential to grow in the future.

Introduce the projections

Given that you are expecting growth in the future, it is a good idea to highlight the relevant facts in an introductory statement on the page before the table. If there is more than one statement I would present them as bullet points. In these introductory statements I draw the reader's attention to the potential growth in the business by demonstrating growth of revenue and margin over a given period.

For example:

• Projected revenue growth over 5 years is 350%

or

• YoY growth: revenue 52%; gross margin 72%

The free spreadsheet from the website will calculate these total and YoY growth figures for you. Note that YoY refers to the growth from one year to the next, rather than the total growth over the entire period (5 years in the example above).

Debt

If your business has any debt it is important to show this in your plan. If you do not show it now it will only come to light later and may give the impression that you are being evasive. Include any debt as a bullet point after the projections table. Explain the nature of the debt in simple terms. For example:

• £50K of debt: 3-year bank loan, 9% per year
• £150K mortgage on commercial premises, 17 years outstanding

There is no need to over-emphasise your business's debt at this stage, or go into too much detail. Just state what the debt amounts to, and its basic terms.

Learn the language of business

The financial section of your plan is fundamental to your business, and the financial numbers are the 'language' in which you can convey its health and potential. Do not avoid the issue just because it might take you out of your comfort zone. Use the spreadsheet I have given you to learn and understand the elements that make up a business in financial terms, and assess how these apply to your own business. If you are still unsure on this point, I recommend that you fill in your assumptions in the spreadsheet and then discuss the results with an accountant or financial analyst. They can check your work and further explain the details of the spreadsheet.

I cannot stress enough how important it is to understand at least the basics of your financial metrics. I have seen many great pitches painfully unravel in response to financial questions. Make sure that you remain a credible investment proposition: spend time learning the language of business.

Example

Fig. 16 is an example Financials page for a business plan. You can see that I have taken the data table and converted it into a graph, which I have placed next to the table. This is in no way essential; it is just a small addition to help emphasise the growth in revenues and margins.

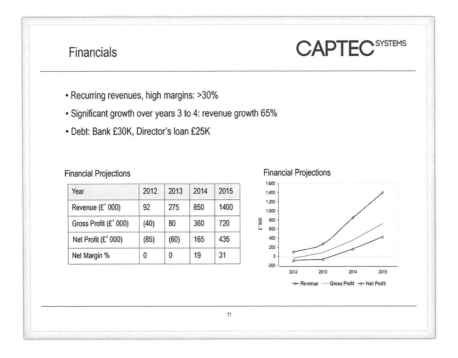

Financials summary:

- Use this page in your plan to demonstrate growth and scale, both future and past.

- Think big, but be realistic. Check that your numbers make sense intuitively and get the help of a professional if necessary.
- Use a table containing only the essential figures and financial metrics. Investors do not want to see too much detail at this point. Think of the table as your bullet points for financials.
- Understand how to arrive at your net profit number via EBITDA. Remember, net profit is after you have paid corporation tax.
- Project between 3 and 5 years into the future, including revenue, gross profit and net profit.
- Include historic figures if relevant and helpful.
- Consider including gross and net margin figures as additional rows in the table. Express these figures as percentages so that the reader can make a quick mental comparison with other businesses in the sector that they might know.
- Use the free spreadsheet to help create your financial numbers for the table.
- Show any debt that your business has.
- Learn the basics of the financials and what they mean. They are the language of business. You will be a much more attractive investment proposition as a result.

CHAPTER 16. INVESTMENT

The function of this page in your plan is very simple: to state how much investment you need and what you are offering in return. You must also show, in very broad terms, how you intend to use this investment. Furthermore, you need to outline any investment that your business has already received.

Valuing your business

Stating your required investment sounds easy enough – but in fact it is a potential minefield. If you come up with the wrong figures, your proposition will fail. To avoid this, you must exercise caution and come up with a realistic valuation for your business.

In stating the amount of a required investment, and what percentage of your business you are prepared to give away in return, you are implicitly placing a valuation on your business as a whole.

Let's say that you are looking for an investment of £100,000. In return you are prepared to give away 10 per cent of the shares in your business. If 10 per cent of your business is worth £100,000, then the valuation you are placing on your business as a whole is ten times that – i.e. £1 million.

This is a catch that causes many entrepreneurs some trouble, in that they tend to overvalue their business. Overvaluation will often mean that a deal does not get done. By 'overvaluation', I mean that the entrepreneur believes that their business is worth more than it really is – or at least significantly more than the value placed upon it by the investors. There is generally a mismatch between these two sets of expectations.

Why does this mismatch happen? Why does the entrepreneur so often exceed sensible levels of valuation when asking for investment? And given this common tendency, how can you arrive at the correct valuation?

It normally comes down to one simple factor: the difference between what a business is worth right now and what it will be worth in the future. If all goes well, a business will usually be worth a lot less today than it will be in several years time, assuming that it is growing.

The problem stems from the fact that an investor will tend to look at what a business is worth now, whereas an inexperienced and perhaps naive business owner will not understand this, and will look just to the future in order to ascertain the business's value. It is thus all too common for there to be a mismatch between what an investor is prepared to pay and what a business owner is prepared to accept, and the opportunity is therefore lost.

The 'proof of concept' that I explained earlier in the book becomes important here, especially for early-stage businesses. If you can demonstrate a working product or service, and also show that people are prepared to pay for it, you have transformed your business from just an idea into a serious investment proposition. This means that not only have you created some value, but there is less risk for an investor because it is clear that the business can make money. Without proof of concept, there is much more uncertainty about whether the business will work, and consequently investors will demand far more in return for investment.

Given that an investor will focus much more on the current valuation of the business than on a future projection, how can you arrive at an investment figure that will be palatable to an investor but also recognise its future potential?

How to value your business

In simple terms, a valuation is usually derived from the profits that you generate. If your business is not yet profitable, then the sales figures are often used instead, as the reference for valuation. As a very rough rule of thumb, you can probably expect to value your business somewhere between five and ten times your net profits after tax (note: not EBITDA, which is before tax). Which end of this spectrum you are on will depend on many factors, such as sector growth, margins, business efficiency, debt levels, assets owned, and so on.

For example, an internet business will have a higher valuation on its profits than a car dealership, as it has significantly more potential for growth. The logic is that if I were to buy or invest in an internet business now, it will probably be more valuable in the future as the profits will be greater, given that the sector is growing quickly as a whole. A car dealership, by contrast, is less likely to grow, and the business is likely to have reached maturity already, so the value placed on the business now will probably be similar to its value in a few years' time.

Take, for example, a business that has profits of £100,000 and no debt. It is in the internet retail space – clearly a growth area, as more consumers are doing more of their shopping online. You could sensibly assume that the valuation of that business is up to ten times current profits, and is therefore around £1 million. This is a simplistic example, and the correct valuation of a business is in fact a highly complex subject – entire careers in the financial sector are devoted to this. But this approach generally represents a sound starting point.

An entrepreneur will inevitably say, with absolute conviction, that in five years' time their business will be making profits of £x. Therefore, in the eyes of the entrepreneur, the business must be worth ten times £x! On the contrary – an investor will appraise the business with greater emphasis on how it is now, rather than in five years' time, and will point out that right now your business is just an idea, or is perhaps generating only a small amount of sales and no profits at all. Therefore, the investor's valuation will usually be significantly lower than that of the business owner.

The trick is to find the middle ground. With the help of proof of concept and the USPs, you will have created some value; but the investor must still be rewarded for taking the risk of investing with you. After all, an investor will always have less risky options for making a return on their money, such as earning interest in a bank account.

Investor's return

The reward for the investor must typically be, at the very least, a doubling of the sum invested over a five-year period. This means that if an investor puts in £100,000 then five years later the investment must be worth at least £200,000, were they to sell their share in the business. Indeed, this doubling of the investment is really an absolute minimum, and many investors will expect a great deal more – usually

110

more like three or four times their original investment as a minimum, in anticipation of tenfold returns, or even more. This level of return may seem high, but there is a risk that the business might fail and this is sadly often the case with many early-stage businesses. Therefore the investor must be rewarded for taking such risk and needs to be able to offset the returns on successful investments against such failures.

A very crude guide to a starting point for a valuation might work like this: take the value that you are attributing to your business in five years' time, and divide it by at least ten. This figure will give you a rough idea of a maximum valuation at which an investor might be willing to invest right now. Clearly, this is very simplistic, but I feel that the concept is valid as a reference point. An analogy is that if your house were worth £250,000, you would not put it on the market for £400,000 just because that is what it might be worth in ten years' time. The reality of the situation is that you are putting it on the market right now – and the same principle holds true for the valuation of a business.

Logical valuation methodology

However you value your business, make sure that you apply a sensible methodology for arriving at that figure. Telling an investor that they should pay the supposed future value of the business today will be seen as nonsense. First of all, there is no guarantee that your projections are correct. Secondly, if an investor is paying a future value today, how can they expect to make money from the investment in the following years?

If you can show that you have valued your business sensibly and that there is a logical rationale behind the figure, you will inspire confidence in an investor and make a more interesting investment prospect in your own right. If you put an unrealistic, over-inflated valuation on your business you will make things much more difficult for yourself.

Having gone through the process of raising capital a number of times myself, I have found it best not to overcook the valuation in the expectation of being negotiated down. Personally, I have always preferred to pitch at a figure that I feel is realistic and fair, and then broadly stick to that number, while perhaps allowing just a little room for negotiation along the way.

Beware of losing control

When you are negotiating the investment it is important to accept that if you are being asked to give up 50 per cent or more of your business it is in fact no longer your business. If you own anything less than 51 per cent of your business you do not have a controlling stake. This is fine for some – especially if it is a large business with a good corporate governance infrastructure, and perhaps if the rest of it is owned by a number of other parties, each with a smaller stake than you. Otherwise you must accept that you will not be able to control the strategic direction of the business, and you are arguably no different from an employee: you will now have a taskmaster who can eject you from the running of the business if they so choose.

Identify investment required

To work out how much investment you need you must work out the costs of your business, and the period over which you expect these costs to apply before they are covered by the revenues that you expect to generate in the future.

You can use the spreadsheet on the website to enter the costs associated with running your business. This will give you a guide to the required investment, as it will show you how much money you need to spend to make the business work, and consequently how much of that needs to come from an investment. Listing your costs is important because you will need this when you explain to an investor what you intend to use their investment for.

Once you have worked out how much investment you require, check it against the valuation you have placed on your business to confirm that it is reasonable. If the investment required is much more than the value of the business you may have a problem – you must either reduce your initial investment requirement or increase the value of your business.

Presentation

When you show the investment that you require on your plan, and what you are offering in return, you must do so concisely in the first two bullet point statements:

- Investment required: £150,000
- Offering 20% equity (valuation £750,000)

Note that 'equity' is quite a broad term in business, but in this context it is synonymous with the concept of ownership of shares in the business. So '20% equity' is the same as saying '20% share ownership'.

Remember that you should always cross-reference the investment you are asking for with your profitability, both present and future, as a way to check that your figures broadly make sense. Make sure that you can explain to an investor why the business is worth what you say it is, so that there is a clear rationale for the level of investment you are seeking.

Prior investment

Now that you have shown how much investment you need, you must state how much investment has already gone into the business, if any. State who made the investments and at what valuation they were made. For example:

- Management own 75%. Invested £100K in 2007.
- Two external investors own 25%. Invested £100K in 2008.

Management must invest

Note that the example states how much the management team has invested. This is an important point that every potential investor will inevitably ask. I have been in many pitches where the answer to this single question can make or break an investment decision, no matter how great the business idea is or how much progress has been made. It is a simple question from the investor to the owner of the business – 'How much have you got in the business?' – and it should in theory yield a simple answer.

The answer to this question is crucial because of what is generally referred to as 'alignment of interests'. This means that an investor will not want to invest in your business and take risk if you, as the owner, do not have some 'skin in the game' as well. Quite rightly, the investor needs to see that you believe in your business enough to risk your own money.

As a business owner you are either fully committed or you are not. I have lost count of the number of times that someone has come asking for an investment – insisting on how talented they are, how successful they have been, what an amazing business they have, and so on – only to respond, when asked 'How much money have you personally invested?' something like: 'Well, I haven't actually put any money in, but I have given up my time…'; or maybe 'I can't put enough in for it to be meaningful to the business' – or some other nonsensical excuse. And that's what answers like this are: excuses. If you aren't prepared to put any of your own money into the business, it sends a clear signal that you are not committed and that you do not really believe in what you are doing.

There are a few exceptions to this: a young entrepreneur who has just left school and has no money of their own behind them, for example. They clearly have no savings or anything to invest themselves, other than their own blood, sweat and tears. This type of 'investment' is often referred to as 'sweat equity'.

Anita Roddick, who founded the ethical retail chain The Body Shop, was a good example of sweat equity. She had no significant money of her own and started selling her products at markets and car-boot sales. To fund her first shop she persuaded a friend to invest, and this kick-started a venture that became the multinational business it is today. But if you are someone with some professional experience and have clearly been well-paid in the past, but are not prepared to put your own money into your own business, think how that will look to an investor! Most importantly, you should not avoid the subject. It is absolutely inevitable that an investor will ask you about your own financial commitment to the business.

Other commitments

Investors will also want to see that you are wholeheartedly focused on the business they are investing in. Commitment is expressed in terms of time and focus as well as money. The investor will therefore ask you about your other professional and work commitments. If you are simultaneously running other businesses in addition to the one for which you are seeking investment, they will usually lose interest.

Use of investment

So far you have articulated how much investment has been made, how much more you are looking for, and what valuation you place on your business. Now you must show an investor what you intend to do with the investment once you have secured it. As with so much else in your plan, this does not need to take the form of a comprehensive list of every detail – that will come later, as an investor becomes more interested and starts taking a closer look. All you need to do for now is provide a snapshot of how the funds will be used. Unlike the financials page, this information does not need to be broken down over a period of years – even if the investment is to be used over a term lasting longer than the first year. Investment will be used for a range of purposes. Typical examples include:

- salaries
- contractor/outsourcing fees
- office space
- marketing and advertising
- product development and manufacture
- machinery or hardware purchase
- stock purchase
- design, print and packaging
- IT systems

On this page of the plan I like to list the uses in bullet points, with the corresponding amount of money applied to each line. For example, the list in Auntie Helen's mop plan might have looked something like this:

- manufacture   £80K
- sales manager salary   £40K
- design   £15K
- warehouse   £12K
- shipping   £5K
- other   £3K

It is important to list only the really meaningful items. If you intend to put some of the investment towards smaller items – telephone expenses, coffee, paper, and so on – these details can be grouped in a general category called 'other', as shown above.

If a large proportion of the investment is for use on a specific item, then it is perfectly acceptable to include the name or description of this item. For example, 'fabric' may be a big part of the investment spend for the Wavecave. Alternatively, it might just be shown as something more generic, such as 'materials', which can then also include smaller items such as tent pegs, poles, shoulder straps, and so on.

Government grants and tax incentive schemes

Finally, if your business qualifies for any government investment incentive schemes it is essential that you briefly mention this fact. Many countries have schemes incentivising private investors to put money into early-stage businesses. Such schemes allow the investor to reclaim from the government some of the money they have invested in your business. This typically means that the investor may claim against any personal tax liabilities that they have. This can make investing in an eligible business very attractive, as the investment is in effect costing the investor less than the amount that they actually put into the business. The logic behind such schemes is that business growth is good for the economy, and so governments want to encourage investors to help businesses get started.

For example, an investor may put £100,000 into your business, but be able to reclaim £30,000 from the government because of the investment incentive scheme. In effect, the £100,000 investment has only cost the investor £70,000.

You will need to talk to an accountant to establish whether your business is eligible for such a scheme, and how to go about getting the necessary certification.

Likewise, if your business has made use of any government grants you should highlight this and state the type of grant and the value.

Example

Fig. 17 on the page opposite shows an example page for the 'Investment' section.

Investment

- Investment required: £250K
- Offering 20% equity (valuation £1.25m)
- Management invested £300K at launch; owns 75% equity
- Angel investor invested £100K in 2010; owns 25% equity
- EIS eligible: 30% tax relief on investment

Use of funds (£ '000s)

- Warehouse expansion: 75
- Vehicles: 100
- New hires / salaries: 50
- Other: 25

12

Investment summary:

- Beware of the mismatch in valuation between investors and entrepreneurs, and ensure that your valuation accounts for the value of the business now, and not just an assumed future value.
- State the amount of investment you need clearly. If you don't ask, you don't get!
- Ensure that the investment requested makes sense relative to your valuation.
- Ask yourself if the valuation allows scope for an investor to make back several multiples of their original investment. Remember: they are investing to make money!
- Clarify any investment made so far.
- It is essential to be clear about how much the management team has invested in the business. The investment of time alone is not acceptable. If you are not prepared to put money into your own business, do not expect others to do so.
- State clearly what you will use the investment for.
- Show any investment incentive scheme for which you have certification.

CHAPTER 17. EXIT

The aim of this page of your business plan is to explain to the investor how you intend for them to recover their original investment plus a decent return. This process is called the 'exit'. The exit is the mechanism by which the investor extracts their capital from your business and makes a profit in the process.

Let's not forget that the reason the investor invests in the first place is to make some money from your business. They are not investing money as a loan, from which they may make a modest return on their investment – and they are not investing on a charitable basis, just because they like you. An investor puts money in your business to make more money: it's as simple as that. If this all sounds too brutally capitalist, then you need to think twice about asking for an investment in the first place, as making money is what investment is all about. In order to make money, the investor must, at some point, be able to cash in their investment – and this is where the exit comes into play.

Failure to mention the exit

I am often surprised by the number of business plans that fail to mention the exit. After all, the plan must be more about the investor's needs than your own. This relates to the service that you are able to offer the investor: by providing some clarity on the question of the exit, you are catering to the investor's needs.

When I see no reference to an exit in a business plan it usually rings alarm bells. It says to me that the entrepreneur or business owner is not thinking things through all the way to the end. So make sure that you include this page in your plan: it is an easy win. It shows that you are 'worldly wise' as a business operator, and demonstrates that you understand what an investor is looking for.

Types of exit

There are typically three mechanisms that offer a potential exit:

1. Trade sale
2. Public listing (also known as an 'IPO')
3. Profit distributions and / or debt repayment

Let's take a look at what each of these means.

Trade sale

This is where you sell your business to another, usually much larger, business. The proceeds are then split between the shareholders on a basis that is proportionate to their ownership. Ideally, the amount that the investor receives from the sale will be far greater than the amount they originally invested.

Public listing

This is also known as an IPO (initial public offering), or 'flotation', and was all the rage during the dotcom boom in the nineties. Rather than selling your shares to another business, you make your shares available for purchase by the 'public' via a stock exchange where they are freely tradable. In reality, although it is called a 'public offering' it is usually large investment institutions such as pension funds and insurance companies that make up the bulk of the buyers of your shares, rather than members of the general public. The price at which your shares are initially made available on the stock exchange will be much higher than the valuation at which the investor originally acquired them. At that point the business would have been far less profitable and much more risky – so now the investor is rewarded for sharing this risk.

Profit distribution and / or loan repayment

It might be the case that neither a trade sale nor a flotation takes place, and this is in fact the most common scenario. As a business continues to grow and become more profitable, an investor is paid back gradually, making a return through the profits generated. When payments are made to the shareholders of a business from the profits in this way they are called dividend payments. This is a valuable mechanism, as it means an investor can recover their initial investment over time while retaining the additional benefit of a potential trade sale or flotation in the future. Sometimes an investment might be made as a loan, but such a deal for early-stage ventures would also usually include some shares in the business (often referred to as 'equity upside' or an 'equity kicker'). The business repays the loan over time, which returns the original amount invested to the investor, and then the investor can enjoy any future dividends safe in the knowledge that the investment is now risk-free.

It might be difficult to know which outcome is the most likely, in the early stages of your business, and it may be some time before it is apparent which is the most viable mechanism for exit. Despite this, rather than simply listing the three options above in your plan you should justify why you think any of them might represent a realistic option.

Justify the exit

The best way to justify a potential exit strategy is to refer to what has happened in the past with similar companies in similar sectors, as well as making reference to current trends. For example, if several companies have undergone trade sales in your sector in recent years I suggest that this should be your identified aim as an exit. In the late nineties, technology companies generally sought public listings as their preferred exit route, and public stock markets saw a dotcom frenzy as a result. At that time a public listing might well have been a realistic exit mechanism to aim for.

Things have moved on since then and, although investors now recognise the internet and technology sectors as established markets with huge potential, some lessons have been learned. Consequently you now see far fewer technology listings than in the heyday of the dotcom boom, and it is typically the larger, better-established firms that seek an IPO. As a result, smaller, fast-growing technology firms tend to seek an exit through a trade sale to these larger, already publicly listed businesses.

In the economic environment at the time of writing (2012), I would suggest that specifying a trade sale as your intended exit makes the most sense, assuming that there are examples of this in your sector already – though if your business is a world-beater, you may feel that you want to go for a public listing, where fortunes can be made (and lost!). If that's the case, and your ambitions know no bounds, then specify an IPO as your form of exit – but make sure you can justify this with examples of recent flotations of similar businesses in similar sectors.

Comparables

When outlining your exit, you should demonstrate similar exits of comparable companies. These are known as 'comparables'. It is important to include reference to comparables, as they show the investor that there is indeed a mechanism in your business sector by which they can crystallise a return on their investment into cold, hard cash.

For example, let's say that I want to start an internet comparison website that focuses on financial products and services. The site will compare and contrast the best prices for insurance products, savings accounts, pension funds, and so on. On this page of your plan you should show a list of comparable businesses that have successfully exited. Be clear about what the exit values and multiples were ('multiples' meaning how many times bigger the exit value was than profits generated for that year).

- moneysupermarket.com floated 2009. Current valuation £600m. Multiple 12x.
- beatthatquote.com trade sale to Google for £38m. Multiple 10x.

In these examples I have only shown exits in the UK, but it is perfectly acceptable, and advisable, to include comparable exits abroad.

At the inception of moneysupermarket.com, someone almost certainly invested just a few hundred thousand pounds for a meaningful stake in the business. Imagine that you invested £100K for 10 per cent when the business started out. Your £100K would now be worth £60 million! That's the power of an exit. Comparable exits will reassure investors that they are not entering a wild goose chase, and also help justify the valuation you place on your business when asking for investment. It is a bit like the 'proof of concept' for your product or service, except that in this case it is more a 'proof of exit', whereby you show that successful exits in your space have been achieved.

If there are no comparable exits – which may be the case if you are a genuine first-mover – then be honest and make that clear. It is not necessarily a bad thing, and may indeed be seen as a potential opportunity, in that you might be the first in your sector to sell out or float.

Potential acquirers

When highlighting a trade sale as your most likely exit, it is essential to list those companies that are likely to acquire your business, especially if they have been acquisitive in the past. Try to be realistic about which companies you name here. If you are a technology company, don't just list the obvious suspects such as Google or Facebook: do your homework on which companies are the big players in the broader sector, and which of them might want to gain access to your particular space through acquisition rather than developing a similar product or service themselves. Talk to industry specialists who understand the landscape, and try to acquire a feel for what might make sense.

Profit distributions

If you feel that profit distributions are the most appropriate mechanism by which investors will make a return, make sure that these payments fit with the projected profits and timeframe in your profit-and-loss statements. This may sound obvious, but it is all too easy to be over-optimistic and create a mismatch between projected profits and projected investor payouts. You should state in your plan the anticipated timeframe in which you intend to make these dividend payments so that the investor has a clear indication of when they will get their money back and start making a return on the investment.

Return

It is important to indicate the potential return that an investor can make. The return is the amount of money that the investor receives upon an exit, in relation to their initial investment. This is usually presented as a 'multiple' of the original investment, and annotated with a multiplication sign to represent by how many times the investment has increased.

For example, let's say an investor makes a £100,000 investment at the outset and the business is sold five years later at a value that means their original stake is now worth £1,000,000. Therefore the investor has made a tenfold return on their investment. This tenfold investment should be shown as '10x' in the business plan.

When you state the potential return, make sure that this number ties in sensibly with your valuation and projections and with any comparable exits.

Ending your plan

Finally, outlining an exit - even if the event is a long way off - makes a fitting conclusion to your business plan. Just as an exit is the logical ending for your business, so it is the case for your plan. Remember that the purpose of your plan is to tell the story of your business so that the investor gets the whole picture as clearly as possible. In the same way that a story needs a clear ending, so does your plan.

Example

Fig. 18 shows how a typical 'Exit' page should look.

Exit   **CAPTEC**SYSTEMS

• Sector with several large, acquisitive incumbents

• Target exit via trade sale early year 5

• Target exit value at £4m (approx 9x EBITDA)

• Return of 8x, based on initial 2012 equity investment of £150K (30% equity)

Comparables

• Protrack bought by Sentinel Systems Inc in 2009 for $22m (12x EBITDA multiple)

• Market Diagnostics Ltd sold to Symtech Plc for $15m, 3 years from inception on 9x

• Broadchamp Ltd sold for £13m on 7x multiple

13

Exit summary:

- Demonstrate the exit to show an investor that you are aware of their needs and have a long-term, strategic view.
- Show comparable exits that have already taken place. This helps to justify both your claims for an exit and also your current valuation; constituting a 'proof of exit', much like a 'proof of concept'.
- Select the most appropriate and likely exit by looking at current trends in your sector, and also at how similar businesses have exited in the past.
- If you specify a trade sale as your most likely exit, you must list the potential acquirers.
- If dividends are your preferred exit, make sure you give a clear timeframe for when the expected distributions will take place.
- Use the Exit page as a coherent, logical conclusion to your plan.

CHAPTER 18. EXECUTIVE SUMMARY REVISITED

Remember that the very first slide of the business plan was called 'Executive Summary'? I explained that this page was a quick snapshot of the contents of the rest of your plan but was best left until the end, when you had written all of the other pages of your plan. This is because the Executive Summary draws on material from the rest of your plan, and then condenses it into the key issues.

As the title suggests, it is a summary and its aim is to enable the reader to understand, within a minute or two, your business proposal and where the commercial opportunity lies for an investor. In effect, this page works as an introduction to the rest of your plan.

If your business plan provides a concise picture of where your business is now and where you intend to go with it, then the Executive Summary is a snapshot of that concise picture.

Essential topics

There are some essential areas that you must address in the Executive Summary, and they can simply be drawn from the headings of each chapter in your plan:

- Background
- USP
- Progress
- Market
- Financials
- Investment
- Exit

To make the Executive Summary effective, you must refer to each page in your business plan and summarise its contents into a single bullet point. If you thought summarising what your business does in one or two pages was difficult, then this is even more of a challenge! But don't worry – you have already done the hard work, and the statements on the 'Executive Summary' page are not meant to be detailed; they should simply give the reader a broad indication of what the rest of the plan will contain.

Example

Fig. 19 is an example of an 'Executive Summary' slide. Note how the points in the slide correspond and relate to the list of essential topics listed previously.

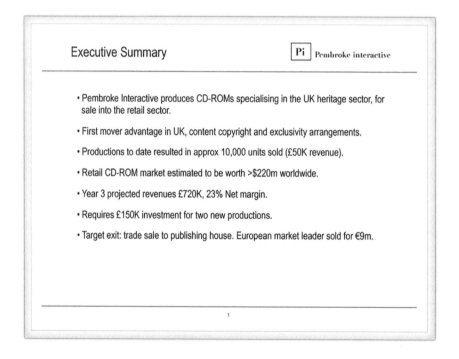

If there is a key consideration that makes your business very appealing, be sure that you include it in the Executive Summary, even if this means adding an extra statement to those listed previously.

Use the pages already created

As a guide to help you compress each relevant page of your plan into a single statement or two, I recommend that you look to the first two or three points of each page in your plan. If you have followed the structure and format that I have recommended, these first few points should give you what you need to create the single statement for the Executive Summary.

For example, let's take a look at the 'Investment' page of your plan. On this page, the first thing that you state is how much investment you are asking for. This therefore corresponds to the 'Investment' statement in your Executive Summary, because here you also need to state the amount of investment you require. Likewise with 'USP' and 'Progress'. The first one or two statements on each of these pages of your plan will always be the most important, and should therefore be reiterated in the Executive Summary.

To highlight this, compare the second line of the example in **Fig.19** to the content of **Fig. 8**, in the 'USP' chapter of this book. It is clear how the two pages relate to one another and that the information in the 'Executive Summary' page is really little more than a short summary of what is said in the 'USP' page.

Executive Summary:

- Give investors a snapshot of your plan. They must be able to understand the broad outline of your proposal within one or two minutes.
- Keep the Executive Summary to an absolute maximum of ten key statements – and aim for fewer.
- Transfer key content from the corresponding pages of your plan, but make it even more concise.
- Make sure that the rationale for investment is clear on this page. This is an opportunity to engage your reader immediately, motivating them to read on.

CHAPTER 19. CONCLUSION

This is the final page of your business plan and its purpose is twofold: first, it creates a clear ending to your plan; second, it acts as a final 'sales pitch'. This sales pitch emphasises the most positive aspects of your business, and aims to leave these points resonating with your investor.

This might sound very similar to the purpose of the Executive Summary at the beginning of your plan – and there are indeed strong similarities between the two. In the same way that the Executive Summary anticipates the important points from various chapters in your plan, the Conclusion should echo the essential elements of what has already been covered in detail.

But there is a fundamental difference. Whereas the Executive Summary serves to introduce the content that is to follow, so that the reader begins with a 'snapshot' of the plan, the Conclusion acts more as a final sales pitch, highlighting your strengths and key selling points.

Different from the Executive Summary

This difference should be clear from the type of language you use. The Executive Summary should be as objective and 'fact-based' as possible – it is essentially a statement of what is to come. By contrast, the Conclusion should use qualifying statements ahead of any summary of content – statements that will underline the positive nature of the points being made. The key difference between the two sections relates largely to the use of these qualifying statements.

There will be other differences between the Conclusion and the Executive Summary. The Conclusion, for example, does not need to comment in any way on what the business does – the reader will already have this information by now.

Relevant chapters

The chapters you should use to generate content for the Conclusion include:

1. USP
2. Progress
3. Market
4. Management
5. Financials
6. Investment
7. Exit

There is one further area that you will need to address in the Conclusion. This relates to the anticipated return that you expect to make for an investor. I will discuss this later in the chapter.

As you will notice, several of the areas that you need to address overlap with those in the Executive Summary. Let's work through each of the sections:

1. **USP** – The area you address here will be much the same as the point you made in your Executive Summary, where you highlighted your key USPs. However, given that you are making a strong 'pitch' here for your business, you should use qualifying language ahead of the USP. For example:

Clear, strong USPs: first-mover advantage and IP

Qualifying statement   *Factual statement*

2. **Progress** – Again, reiterate the essential content of the relevant chapter in your plan and show your key progress to date.

Clear proof of concept: sales of £50K in year 1

Qualifying statement   *Factual statement*

3. **Market** – State the size of the market and any marked growth. You should emphasise the fact that the market is big enough to be of interest to an investor, and that there is enough growth to lift your business with the 'rising tide'.

   • Large, growth market: $3bn, growing 15% per year

4. **Management** – Use a single statement to highlight the most relevant experience or expertise that the management has – for example: 'Over 80 years' direct, collective experience in the sector'. A qualifying statement such as 'Highly experienced management team' will work to emphasise this point.

5. **Financials** – As in the Executive Summary, highlight the one or two most important financial metrics. Qualifying statements might include 'Strong financial growth (followed by the relevant figures)' or 'High-margin business with growth'.

6. **Investment** – State the amount of investment required, and give a broad, 'big picture' rationale for the need for the investment. Keep the reason for the investment upbeat and positive. For example:

   • £150K investment needed to take business to the next stage of growth

   or

   • £150K investment required to bring business to profitability

7. **Exit** – If it is the case, state the fact that there is a clear exit. Follow this with the most likely type of exit, and make clear that there have been comparable exits on attractive valuations.

   • Clear exit strategy for trade sale in 5 years, demonstrated by comparable exits on valuations of > 8x

8. **Return** – It is important that you state the return you expect an investor to make, based on the relationship between their initial

investment and the amount at which they will exit the business (or receive dividend distributions). Work from the figures that you presented in your 'Exit' page.

Example

Fig. 20 shows an example conclusion page for the Paper Pallet Company.

Conclusion   THE**PAPER**PALLET**CO.**

- **Clear USP's**: first-mover and IP ownership
- **Proven concept**: > 50,000 units selling per month
- **Scalable market**: > £750m in UK
- **Experienced management**: team have worked entire careers in paper and packaging sector, with successful trade sale exit experience
- **Strong financials**: explosive revenue growth at > £5m in year 2
- **Investment**: £1m required to scale sales effort and drive to profitability
- **Sound exit strategy**: sector with several large blue-chip firms, with proven appetite for acquisition of early-stage innovators; sector comparables of 6x – 15x
- **Compelling returns**: return on investment potential at 10x over 4 years

14

Conclusion summary:

- Use this chapter to bring your plan to a clearly defined endpoint.
- Ensure that the tone is upbeat and positive.
- List the key statements that make up your selling points. Draw them from the relevant chapters in your plan, much as you did in the Executive Summary.
- Make the page your 'sales pitch'. The use of positive qualifying statements that emphasise the key selling points of your business can help to achieve this. This will ensure that the reader finishes the plan with these points resonating in their mind.

PART 3

NEXT STEPS

CHAPTER 20. GET YOUR INVESTMENT

Congratulations! You have finished your plan. Perhaps you have even achieved basic proof of concept on your business, and your financial numbers are stacking up nicely. You are excited about the future and how your business can grow. So what next? What are you going to do with your plan? Who do you take it to in order to get your investment and how do you go about that?

Who to approach

Once you have your plan and are ready to ask for an investment, the obvious next question is who you should approach with it. You may have a few people in mind already, but in order to succeed you will usually need to cast your net far wider than your existing direct relationships and contacts.

There are typically three types of investors who might be open to investing in return for a stake in your business:

1. Friends and family
2. Angel investors
3. Venture capitalists

Friends and family

Friends and family will have provided your early support, and are obviously people you already know. They will typically invest small amounts, alongside your own investment, to help get you going at an early stage. They are often invaluable in helping you pull together the funding that you need to kick-start your business.

Angel investors

Angel investors are usually wealthy individuals who make direct investments in early-stage businesses with the aim of exiting later, having recovered a multiple of this original investment. They will often have started businesses themselves, and this is usually the source of their wealth. Consequently they have a good deal of business experience and expertise. Angel investors can therefore be a very valuable source of help to your business and will often take a surprisingly keen interest in your progress. They can be fantastic investors to have on board and are often very understanding of the pressures and difficulties of growing a business, since they have probably done it themselves. Their investment will usually fall between £10,000 and £150,000, though it might occasionally be more.

Venture capitalists

Venture capitalists make investments in businesses on a professional basis and it is their raison d'être. Their investment level is usually much higher than the other types of investor – typically well in excess of £250,000, and often in the millions. Consequently, they rarely invest in very early-stage businesses. They will almost certainly want to see some meaningful proof of concept, or at the very least a highly experienced and complete management team. They will expect clear financial information and comprehensive data on markets, opportunities, competition, and so on. In short, they will expect you to have done your homework thoroughly, and to have a detailed understanding of your sector and the opportunity you have identified within it.

New sources

A further source of funding can be found through the internet via crowdfunding and peer-to-peer lending websites. These are a relatively new phenomenon, but they are becoming increasingly popular very quickly and showing explosive growth. They are based on the idea that pitches for investment are made to the general public through the crowdfunding website. Such websites include Kickstarter, Indiegogo, Seedrs, Crowdcube and so on. There are many sites that operate in this sector and they often focus on a particular areas ranging from start-up funding through to more mature B2C debt and equity funding. A simple Google search will list the funding platforms. This is potentially a great new source of funds and I believe it has huge potential and is well worth considering when raising investment.

Making contact

So how do you find and make contact with angel investors and venture capitalists? Well, the latter are easy. There are venture capital associations in most countries that will provide comprehensive national lists of venture capitalists and even a cursory internet search will also provide a range of leads and contacts.

To reach angel investors, usually the best approach is to go through an angel network. An angel network is the single point of contact for a large group of angel investors, and is by far the most efficient and effective way of getting in front of them. The network will usually help you to prepare your business plan, and will offer feedback from experienced investors before you present to the network as a whole. A network will often give you access to many more angel investors than you would otherwise find by yourself. For example, I regularly attend the Oxford Investment Network's monthly meetings, where five or six businesses will present to more than fifty angel investors in one go.

Contacts provided

To help get you moving as quickly as possible, I have provided a list of venture capitalists, investors and angel networks in a downloadable pack from the book's accompanying website (www.businessplansthatgetinvestment.com). You may find this helpful as a starting point.

Move fast

Your primary objective is to use your plan to 'get your foot in the door' and develop some sort of initial dialogue with an investor. Therefore, when an investor asks to see your plan, you should make sure that it reaches them as soon as possible.

I recently had a conversation with the founder of an anti-virus software company, which he sold for more than £100 million. He told me that as an active angel investor the two things that he immediately looks for in a business plan are how quickly it is sent to him after he requests to see it and how many spelling mistakes it contains! If the response is slow or the plan has spelling mistakes, he will reject the proposal. So the message is clear: always check your spelling, and respond swiftly to requests.

Covering 'letter' and follow up

When you email the PDF of your plan to an investor, keep the covering content of your email brief – literally just a few lines. Let the plan do the talking. Once you have sent the plan, if you hear nothing after a few days, I suggest that you follow up with a phone call. Calling someone you do not know is always easier said than done – but it can be very effective, and can push your business to the front of the investor's mind, and your plan to the top of the pile. Indeed, I'd go as far as to say that just by making the phone call you are already differentiating yourself from the pack of other applicants, many of whom will not do so. It is sometimes true that those who shout loudest get heard!

Once an investor has received and read your plan, and then expressed further interest, the next step will usually be a face-to-face meeting. Here the expectation will be that you talk through the plan and the investor will put questions to you about your business. At this point the plan takes on a second function, providing an excellent prompt for a discussion. Never be shy of referring back to the plan in conversation – especially if you get stuck, or (like me) are not so good at remembering facts and figures!

Due diligence

After the initial meeting, if the investor is still interested, they will ask for more information, perhaps introduce you to their colleagues and do their own homework on your business and the sector.

This work, often known as 'due diligence', may include checking your financials, confirming patents, confirming investments you have made in your own business, checking sales figures, and so on. From this point the process usually takes on a momentum of its own and can ultimately lead to an expression of intent to invest, followed by the preparation of any necessary draft contracts, term sheets or agreements.

Throughout this time, if you sense that an investor is seriously interested, try to stay in regular contact. Obviously you do not want to appear desperate or inappropriate – but you must not let the trail go cold, so as to stay at the forefront of their mind.

Once the preparation of a term sheet or draft contract is underway, the due diligence process will inevitably take a significant step up in pace, and the level of scrutiny and detail required about you and your business will become more detailed and intensive.

Closing the deal

As the due diligence process is nearing its end, you will get to the point where you actually close the deal, and get the money in your bank account. This can often be the hardest part of the entire investment process and there are usually a few false dawns, where agreed deadlines, and sometimes the valuation itself, may well miss targets and get moved. Don't let this sort of thing unsettle you – it is par for the course. At this stage in the process it is essential to stay calm and patient and continue to work with the investor with a positive frame of mind in order to help them get their due diligence process complete and watertight, so that the investment can go ahead.

CHAPTER 21. CONCLUSION

Writing a business plan and raising investment can seem incredibly difficult at the outset. Hopefully I have helped you understand that this does not need to be the case, and that it is in fact far less daunting than it might otherwise seem. With many things in life, the first step is often the hardest, and writing a business plan is no different. But I guarantee you that once you have started writing your plan and taken that first step, the rest of the plan will come naturally, and you will find it an enjoyable and exciting experience.

Once you have begun, you should aim to focus and commit to writing your plan through to completion promptly; and always ensure that it meets investors' needs before your own.

Above all, follow the structure I have given you and make it your own. The structure is the key to success. Use it as the starting point for your plan and as the roadmap to its overall content.

Finally, I wish you the very best of success with your plan and your quest for investment.

Good luck and Godspeed!

VISIT

www.businessplansthatgetinvestment.com

TO ACCESS THIS BOOK'S SUPPLEMENTARY MATERIAL, INCLUDING A MODEL BUSINESS PLAN TEMPLATE, KEY CONTACT LIST AND MORE